32 YEARS OF TITLES AND TEARS FROM THE BEST SEAT IN THE HOUSE

WHAT I LEARNED ABOUT HAPPINESS, GREATNESS, LEADERSHIP AND THE EVOLUTION OF SPORTS SCIENCE

Gary Vitti

ICON Sports Publishing
32 Years of Titles and Tears from the Best Seat in the House
What I Learned about Happiness, Greatness, Leadership
and the Evolution of Sport Science

Published in the United States by
ICON Sports Publishing
871 Coronado Center, Suite 200
Henderson, NV 89014

ISBN: 9781686866708
Cover Design by Jorge Hernandez
Cover Photo: Andrew D. Bernstein/ Getty Images
Back Cover Photo: Andrew D. Bernstein/Getty images

FORWARD

FORWARD

I was on track in the summer of 1984 to spend the rest of my professional life in academia. I had just spent the last two years setting up a sports medicine program at the University of Portland. I designed their soon-to-open $7 million state-of-the-art arena's athletic training center and drew up the teaching curriculum. The plan was to finish my Ph.D., teach, do research, and impart my knowledge to the athletic community. Then one hot August day I received a call from the LA Lakers asking if I would be interested in becoming the Lakers head athletic trainer. Flattered that the NBA's flagship franchise was interested in me but reluctant to leave the academic world, I agreed to fly to LA and at least explore the opportunity.

What transpired over the next 32 years was an extraordinary experience where I saw first-hand life transform into lessons and lessons learned from life by some of the greatest champions the world has ever seen. I have not only seen this from their athletic prowess but their personal lives as well.

I don't know how to put 32 years in a few pages, but my goal is to give you what my daughters call GV Gems. You may not be a Lakers fan or a basketball fan or even a sports fan, but these gems can apply to anyone's life.

CHAPTER 1
THE MISSION

Memorial Day Weekend 1985

I wake up Saturday, two days before we take on the World Champion Boston Celtics in game one of the NBA Finals. It's the most eagerly anticipated re-match since Muhammad Ali vs. Joe Frazier.

It's taken us nine months to get to this point. We had to play eight pre-season games, 82 regular-season games, and three rounds of the playoffs. Now we are facing the ultimate challenge. We have played the Celtics in the Finals 8 times and lost to them all eight times – including last year. We had the better team, but they somehow overcame the talent gap and beat us in a winner-take-all 7th game that wasn't decided until the last minute.

I'm the Head Athletic Trainer for the Los Angeles Lakers, a job I'm honored and thrilled to have. This is an iconic franchise, similar to the New York Yankees in baseball, the Pittsburgh Steelers in football and Manchester United in soccer. I had previously worked for another pro basketball team, the Utah Jazz, as an assistant athletic trainer while I was in graduate school. That was a good experience, but that was nothing like being with a team on a mission. The intensity and attention that has been surrounding the Lakers from the first day of training camp have been grueling. Now that we are in the Finals, the pressure has gone up exponentially. My bosses are General Manager Jerry West and Head Coach Pat Riley – one already in the Hall of Fame and the other headed there. The team captains are Magic Johnson, and Kareem Abdul-Jabbar – both of them also headed for the Hall of Fame. I am surrounded by greatness on all sides, and I am just a rookie athletic trainer. But I feel like I belong here because I have worked so hard on my mission, which was to be the best I can be, and this is my reward. My friends and family think working for the Lakers is all glitz and glamour. It's not. The job has a

2

hold on me 24/7, and the stress is unreal. I go to sleep at night with a scratch pad on my nightstand, so when I wake up in the middle of the night with some job-related detail on my mind, I can write it down and not forget it in the morning. There's no margin for error when you're trying to win a championship.

Coach Riley is famous for his intensity and attention to detail. He pushes everyone hard, but he has earned my everlasting respect because he sets the tone by working harder than anyone else. He treats everyone with respect. I have never seen him embarrass anyone – unlike some other coaches, I've worked with. Trying to earn his respect motivates me even more than beating the Celtics does. Sometimes in the NBA, you wake up wondering where you are. It's an occupational hazard when you are traveling with the Lakers. The team is like a rock band with fans gathered outside the hotel day and night just to get a glimpse of the players or an autograph from one of the stars.

For eight months of the year, we spend half our time in LA and half in other cities that have none of the reliable warmth and lush splendor of LA. We fly commercially and can rarely get a flight out of town after a game. Typically, I'm wired and wide awake after a game, so a good night's sleep is out of the question. Then we wake up before dawn to catch the first flight out to the next city. After a few months of this, you often become numb to where you are.

But this morning there's no wondering where I am. I'm in Boston, home of the hated Celtics - our arch-nemesis. Not just our rivals. Our nemesis. We've never beaten them when it matters. That's why everyone in the Lakers organization hates the Celtics. Jerry West, who lost six NBA Finals to the Celtics when he was one of the greatest players in league history, refuses to wear anything green, which he often refers to as "Celtic green. It's my first year with the Lakers, so this is my first time in the Finals. The first time I'm feeling the intense emotion surrounding it. The first time I feel the hatred coming from both sides. But it feels right and natural to me. Like it's been a part of me forever.

I grew up outside metropolitan New York in Stamford, Connecticut. As a kid in the 1960's and '70's, I was a die-hard New York sports fan. Knicks, Giants, Rangers, and Yankees: I rooted for them all. The flip side of that is hating everything Boston: Celtics, Bruins, Patriots, Red Sox, even Boston College, and Boston University teams. It was so ingrained in me that I never even met a Celtic fan before attending Southern Connecticut State University in New Haven. That was the Mason Dixon line for the Boston-New York rivalry. Fans living north of New Haven rooted for Boston teams and hated their New York rivals. Those living south of New Haven rooted for New York teams and hated their Boston rivals.

And beyond my love for the New York teams, I always rooted for the Lakers – except when the Knicks beat them in the 1970 and '73 Finals, and also when they beat the Knicks in the '72 Finals. I was a Lakers fan mainly because I was a huge Jerry West fan. He made the All-Star team 14 times, was known as Mr. Clutch and was the only NBA player to be voted the finals MVP on a losing team. A slim 6-foot-4, his hair always perfectly coiffed and combed even in the heat of battle, he sported a Roman nose that had been broken seven times and the most intense, deep-set pair of hazel eyes I had ever seen. He was humble, hardworking, played through injuries, and was known as the best sportsman in the league. Even the Celtics play-by-play announcer Johnny Most, a chain-smoking, gravel-voiced, nickname giving, mean-spirited homer who never missed an opportunity to bash an opposing player, called him Gentleman Jerry. His basketball form and technique were so classic, so text-book perfect, that the NBA based their logo on a picture of him dribbling the ball. I've spent the last ten months on a mission. Living, working and dreaming about this re-match with players like Magic, Kareem, Jamaal Wilkes, Bob McAdoo, and James Worthy – all on the express train to the Hall of Fame. The Lakers are not just their stars. Role players like power forward Kurt Rambis, the first big-money free agent Mitch Kupchak, lock-down defender Michael Cooper, famed college point guard Ronnie Lester, sharpshooters Byron Scott and Mike McGee, board banger Larry Spriggs and the human toothpick, 7-foot-5 Chuck Nevitt are just as dedicated to beating the Celtics.

They are all finely tuned athletic machines that make them the best athletes in the world. Tall. Quick. Strong. Powerful. Agile. I have gotten to know their hearts and minds too. They are all united in a single goal, a mission. As Coach Pat Riley often says, it's 12+2+1 – 12 players, two coaches and one athletic trainer. We are the inner sanctum, the ones on the court or the bench during the heat of competition. Everyone else outside that 15-member circle is referred to as what Riley calls a "peripheral opponent" -- someone who will distract us from our mission to beat the Celtics.

Riley's insistence on keeping the 12+2-1 restricted to those fighting in the trenches every day is a little outdated. Since he was a player, teams have added a second assistant coach. So in reality it's 12 + 3 + 1. That second assistant is not always with the team though. He has a dual role as an advance scout. His job is to watch our next opponent and prepare a report on how to counter their strengths and attack their weaknesses. Dave Wohl is that guy for the Lakers. He's good at his job and provides us with a lot of important information. He's on the road a lot scouting but tries to get back for practices and games.

The media, in Riley's view, are peripheral opponents. Even the beat writers who are around the team every day are put in that category. Most of them are good guys just trying to do their job of chronicling our ups and downs. They're guys that we often travel, drink and dine with, yet they can never be part

5

of that 12+2+1 inner circle. The separation even applies to our friends and family, our wives, and significant others. Crazy as it sounds, they are considered peripheral opponents as well. At least during the eight-month NBA season and never more so than during the Finals. That's when we live inside a cocoon focused completely on the team and the mission.

This will be the ninth time the Lakers play the Celtics in the NBA Finals. The Celtics won all eight previous times, starting in 1962 and culminating in last year's Finals. That's when they beat us in an epic 7-game series that sent the entire Lakers franchise – players, coaches and front office – into a summer-long mass depression. The Lakers' frustration level was off the charts. We were sure we had the better team and should have won, setting off a summer of celebration. But instead, we suffered a summer of pain and humiliation. In the papers the Celtics power forward Kevin McHale, who fancies himself a jokester, labeled us the "Fakers" and called Magic Johnson "Tragic" Johnson. He was called Tragic because he was so depressed over the loss and the uncharacteristic mistakes – unforced turnovers, missed foul shots -- he made at crucial times. Johnson was so shell-shocked he refused to come out of his Bel-Air mansion for a month.

We were mocked and humiliated on radio and TV. The images of Celtics' bench-warmer M.L. Carr waving his victory towel at us and versatile Celtics forward Cedric "Cornbread" Maxwell talking trash at us as they celebrated their game 7 victory were played over and over. There was no escape. Certainly not inside Magic's mansion. After that heartbreaking loss, it's hard to deny that Boston, with its constant talk of Celtic pride and a leprechaun that lurks in the Boston Garden, has some crazy curse on us. That's why the entire Lakers franchise is so fixated on the mission to beat Boston once and for all this year. What I sense – but don't tell them because I'm new on the job – is that the real opponent is not the Celtics but the Lakers ourselves. By any objective standard, we have the

6

better team -- better athletes and more great players. But the players will have to overcome their own doubts and fears before they can defeat the Celtics. The Celtics are in our heads. In my silent opinion, the Lakers need a mind shift. As Joseph Campbell writes in one of my favorite books, the Hero's Journey: "It is only when a man tames his own demons that he becomes king of himself if not of the world."

Now that opportunity to tame our demons and become king of our world is right in front of us. All we have to do is grab it. We are on a mission to prove there will be no more beat downs from a franchise that has tortured us mentally, physically, and emotionally for more than two decades.

****

As I lay in bed, my thoughts drift back one year. Twelve months ago I was watching the '84 Lakers vs. Celtics Finals on TV at my home in Portland. I was working at the University of Portland, where I had spent the last two years setting up its sports medicine program. Now a year later, I'm in the middle of this massively hyped re-match that has attracted hordes of media from all over the country and all over the world. The media can't get enough of the simple storyline of the blue-collar, hardworking, steak-and-potatoes Celtics versus the popped collar, quiche-and-white-wine, sun-surf-and-sand guys from Hollywood.

Hard versus soft.

Grit and grind versus glitz and glamour.

It sounds insightful.

It even sounds true.

But it isn't. Not if you look beneath the surface. Coach Riley contributes to the misperception with his sleek Hollywood image: long, slicked-back hair, clean-shaven, alpha-male face, Italian loafers, and custom-tailored Italian suits. What isn't seen is he is just as demanding with his long practices and fanatical devotion to running and fitness as Celtics Coach KC Jones. The Celtics take great pride in their Irish heritage, but Riley is Irish to the core and just as tough and feisty as anyone on the Celtics or indeed in the entire league.

That blue-collar vs. white-collar angle is the accepted narrative once it enters the media echo chamber. The newspaper writers pass it on to the TV guys and then it's picked up by the national magazine writers who produce their preview pieces for the Finals. The featured players are our great point guard Magic Johnson and the Celtics forward Larry Bird, voted the NBA's Most Valuable Player last season and just announced as the MVP for this season too. Magic is the better playmaker and defender. Bird is the better shooter and rebounder. But their similarities are more striking than their differences. Both are 6-foot-9. Both are great passers. Both are natural-born leaders and ultimate competitors. Both make their teammates better with an unselfish style of play that is contagious. To make matters even more contentious, Magic and his Michigan State team beat Bird and his Indiana State team for the 1979 NCAA championship in the most-watched game in college hoops history. Magic led the Lakers to NBA titles in 1980 and 1982. Bird led the Celtics to NBA titles in 1981 and 1984. It's as if the basketball Gods willed it and put Magic on the Lakers and Bird on the Celtics to continue their personal competition.

This Bird-Magic rivalry had saved the NBA from the malaise it had drifted into during the late 1970s when drugs – especially cocaine – took over the league. Several stars played like all they cared about was collecting the paycheck they needed to buy their nose candy. The press wise guys said the only time most teams played hard was during the last two minutes of the game. Finals games were not shown on live TV over most of the nation. Even the legendary Game 6 of the 1980 NBA

8

Finals, when super-rookie Magic led the Lakers to his first NBA title by scoring 42 points with 15 rebounds and eight assists – thought by many to be the greatest performance ever in a Finals game, rookie or veteran -- wasn't televised live on the west coast. As the '80s got underway and the Celtics and Lakers alternated winning titles with only Philadelphia breaking up the rotation in 1983, fan interest picked up exponentially year by year. This year fan interest has exploded as the Lakers-Celtics rivalry has gone international, with fans all over the world taking sides. Now all the games are being broadcast live everywhere on CBS, the premier network of the big three broadcast networks. It is the golden era of basketball, and I'm right in the middle of it.

****

I'm here in Boston thanks to a most unlikely series of events. It started with an out-of-the-blue phone call from Jerry West's office in August 1984 asking if I was interested in the job of Lakers Athletic Trainer. West and Riley knew I had worked as an assistant athletic trainer with the Utah Jazz a couple of years earlier. Lakers Assistant Coach Bill Bertka had mentioned me as the kind of guy they were looking for. Someone young. Someone on the cutting edge of the emerging sports-medicine revolution that melds nutrition, strength training, and fitness with the more traditional medical aspects of the job.

There have always been athletic trainers, workout gurus, medicine men – call them whatever you want. Athletic trainers go back to the era of the Roman gladiators more than 2,000 years ago. And for most of that time their skills and their tool kit to help athletes were largely unchanged: endless running to get them in shape, starve them to lose weight, have them eat big slabs of red meat to get them strong, and apply lots of heat and ice to heal their sore and strained muscles.

But now in the mid-1980s, science is becoming a bigger and

bigger factor. It is changing the role and the function of athletic trainers. I wanted to be a big part of that evolution. My mission was to lead a research center like the one the University of Portland wanted to build under my direction. I saw myself setting the innovation agenda for sports teams and athletic trainers around the country and maybe even around the world.

Being the head athletic trainer for a professional sports team was not my mission. I was happy in my college work. I was about to be put in charge of a brand-new sports medicine program, complete with a $7-million-dollar, state-of-the-art facility. I was already working on the sports medicine curriculum. The facility was going to have a human performance laboratory, a new athletic training room, and a new weight room.

Frankly, I saw my future in some classroom teaching athletes how to improve their performance — not sitting on a pro sports team's bench, keeping track of timeouts and dealing with injured players. But still, this is the Lakers calling me. THE glamour franchise in THE glamour city. So I agreed to come to LA and talk about it. Why not at least explore the opportunity?

I was surprised and impressed when the Lakers front office sent me a first-class ticket for the flight from Portland to LA. I had never flown first-class before. I flew into LAX and was picked up by Jerry West in a navy blue Mercedes with a tan interior. I had never been in a Mercedes before, and Jerry West was driving it. I started to feel like I was on a magic carpet ride. My childhood idol was going to drive me to the Fabulous Forum! He looked exactly as I remembered him: cool, calm, and collected. Put together.

As a New York Knicks fan, I had watched with equal parts horror, fascination and admiration as West nailed a 63-foot shot at the buzzer to send game three of the 1970 NBA Finals into overtime. The only reason it didn't win the game was that

10

the NBA hadn't yet adopted the three-point shot. I could still see him launching the shot in my mind's eye. I could still picture Knicks players in shock and disbelief as the ball swished through the net. I could still see the howling home crowd at the sold-out Fabulous Forum exploding in joy.

Now, fourteen years later, West is one of the smartest and most successful executives in league history. I can't believe he is taking the time to pick up a potential employee at the airport. I recognize him instantly. We shake hands, and I begin to realize how special this is, and suddenly, I might want this job.

He drives me to the Fabulous Forum in Inglewood. The building is buzzing with excitement as it prepares to host the 1984 Summer Olympic Gold Medal game between Spain and the United States a few hours later. I get caught up in the Olympic fever building throughout the day. I feel like this is all just a crazy dream. That I'm on a journey down the yellow brick road of hoops. That any moment I'll wake up back in Portland.

Instead, I have six hours of talks with West and Riley. I realize the Lakers are on a mission and that mission is to beat the Boston Celtics. We cover everything. Nutrition. Strength training. Flexibility. Sports Psychology of how to motivate the modern athlete. Riley comes across as a progressive, forward-thinking guy always looking for an edge. He wants to know how I would train individual players to maximize their potential. The conversation went like this.

GV: We use something we call the periodization model. You figure out where you are with a player. And where you want to go. We do certain kinds of physical testing. Then we interpret the tests. There are three things you have to look at when you're talking about science. One, tests have to be valid. Make sure it does what we say it does. If we put you on a scale and it says you weigh 200 pounds, you get off for five seconds and then get back on, and it says 200 pounds again,

11

now we have reliability. But if you get back on and it says 195 pounds, where did the other five pounds go? It's an unreliable piece of equipment. It's a simple explanation but it gets the point across (Riley starts nodding slowly in agreement) So we need validity, reliability, and also practicality. Is the information practical? The information can be valid and reliable, but sometimes we can't really use it. So it has to be practical too. Conventional wisdom in the NBA is that lifting weights is a bad idea. Players tell each other they will lose their shooting touch if they bulk up with muscle. Most athletic trainers share that opinion and steer players away from weights. But Riley believes in it and wants someone who can motivate the players to lift weights. And teach them to do it properly.

Riley: How would you get the players to buy into strength training?
GV: We're not going to just put people in the weight room and have them randomly lift weights. We're going to figure out where they are and where we want them to go. What position are they going to play? Is the guy going to be a power forward? Then he has to be heavy enough and strong enough to play against guys like Rick Mahorn. You have to design the individual program for each person. Each program is different. (Again, Riley starts nodding in agreement.) Then we have to talk about the taper.

We train you, but then we taper off your training to maximize your performance. So once we get to where we want to be, we get them to taper off, so they're ready to perform in the game. If a guy is competing for the gold medal in the marathon, you don't want him to run 20 miles the day before the marathon. This is the first time Riley, known for pushing players harder and harder physically and mentally, has ever considered the concept of tapering off as something that could provide a competitive edge. Then I introduce a concept that really catches his attention.
GV: With all training, eventually you reach a point of diminish-

12

ing returns. No matter how much more we keep putting into the equation and developing the player, we don't get anything more in return. Once we reach that point of diminishing returns, that's when we want to stop and recover. And get ready for the next workout.

Riley (staring intently): Point of diminishing returns, huh? (He writes it down. Later, during the season, I hear him use it several times.) He's definitely interested in hiring me. He says he likes me because I'm young, innovative and haven't been scarred by the daily grind of the NBA. He said he could mold me into what he wants me to be. He is on a mission to beat Boston and has identified the training room as an area that could be an advantage over Boston. Every little bit of an edge helps.

Although I feel like I'm on a magic carpet ride, intellectually it still isn't what I want to do with my life. My mission was to be in front of a classroom, not on a team's bench. I'm still not convinced this is the job for me. Towards the end of the interview I told Pat about my plans to finish my Ph.D. and continue my research, Riley utters the 20 most important words of my professional life, a mission changer: "*You can do everything you want to do, but you can do it here with the greatest athletes in the world.*"

Still, it will be West who does the actual hiring. So my final session is alone with West in his office. He asks me what kind of salary I am looking for, what I think the job is worth. Combining my University of Portland's salary with some other part-time jobs, I am making around $25,000. So I ask for $35,000. I figure he will never go that high. That will help me make what is shaping up as a very tough choice that will affect the rest of my life. I am wrong.

West: I'll give you $37,000 a year and a three-year contract with incremental raises. I'm stunned. For the first time, this whole thing is starting to seem real. The job. The quick move I would have to make from Portland to LA. The switch from the classroom to the locker room, changing the mission. The hook is in my mouth, and I am biting hard.

But I still have one major concern. I am a die-hard sports fan who knows that coaches, players, and executives are fired, let go or "part ways" with their teams every day. I had been on the Utah Jazz bench at the Jazz-Lakers game the night the Lakers fired Head Coach Paul Westhead early in the 1981-82 season. It was little more than a year after he had coached the Lakers to the 1980 NBA title. I had seen up close just how unstable pro sports employment could be. So I want to know who I will be reporting to. Who will command my ultimate loyalty? The players? The coach? Or the general manager?

West: I'm going to let Pat make the final hiring decision because he's the guy that's going to have to work with the trainer. But if you get the job – and I hope you do because I like you—I want you to remember one thing (leans back in his chair and pounds his chest with one hand): I'm the boss.

On that encouraging note, I leave his office to fly back to Portland. I've changed my mind. Now I really want the job. I want to be part of the Lakers' mission. The only problem is that instead of West driving me back to LAX, now they tell me to go across the street to some seedy hotel and take its crappy airport shuttle. No more West to drive me around. No more Mercedes.

On the shuttle bus, I have a severe moment of self-doubt. Does the change in my transportation status mean they aren't as interested in me as I am in them? It's the old story: the more you want something, the more anxious you are about getting it. Like the Lakers wanting to beat the Celtics so badly, they keep getting in their own way. Now it is me who has to overcome my doubts and demons to get where I want to go.

14

Back in Portland, I spend an uneasy two days waiting for a decision. Finally West calls to offer the job. I immediately accept.

****

By Labor Day I had moved to LA and found a place in a little seaside suburb called Manhattan Beach. Suddenly I'm living a few blocks from the ocean and working for the coolest pro sports franchise in the world in pursuit of a mission.

I was used to going to work every day, but it is still the NBA off-season, and the Lakers do not have their own practice facility. So there is no place for me to go except the Forum, where West and owner Dr. Jerry Buss and some other Lakers execs have offices. One day I meet power forward Kurt Rambis, a quirky guy famous for his Clark Kent-style black glasses, long hair and a mustache big enough to match my own. Another day I meet reed-thin guard Michael Cooper, the Lakers' best defender. Magic Johnson's pal. A third-round draft choice that developed into the NBA Defensive Player of the Year. But these are just brief here's-the-new-athletic-trainer introductions. There are no organized team activities for me to participate in. So I start hanging out with Josh Rosenfeld, the Lakers' public relations guy. One day West comes into Rosenfeld's office and asks what the hell we are doing there. He tells us to go home and enjoy some time off. When training camp opens, we are going to be on the job all day, every day.

West throws us out of the Forum! It doesn't bother me at all because I have so much respect for him. As the months and years go by, that respect only grows. I gradually realize that West is the team's main pillar, the foundation of the franchise.

His door is always open to me, and I always know I can trust him, no matter what I tell him. Technically he's not part of Riley's 12+2+1 inner circle. But he's the guy who fills all 15 slots in the 12+2+1. He's the guy that we count on to fix the inev-

15

itable problems that are going to crop up when you have 15 strong and sometimes volatile personalities working in such close quarters under such intense pressure to succeed every day.

A couple of weeks later I'm watching Magic, Worthy and Byron Scott practice fast breaks at the Lakers training camp at College of the Desert in Coachella Valley. I have one thought as they zoom up and down the court flicking laser-beam passes with the ball rarely touching the floor: They run like thoroughbreds, slim and sleek and faster than the wind. I have never seen anything like it.

For the first time, I understand that the Showtime style of ball the Lakers are famous for isn't just something that happens spontaneously. They actually practice the fast break every day. Riley instructs Worthy, a 6-foot-9 forward with the quickness and agility of a man 6 inches shorter, and Byron Scott – a 6-foot-5 shooting guard with great hops and a bulls-eye jumper -- to fill the lanes while Magic grabs the outlet pass and motors up the court looking to pass to one of them or take the ball all the way to the hoop himself. I notice that Worthy runs out of bounds on the sideline to give himself a better angle before he starts cutting for the basket. Cooper or Scott do the same thing on the other side of the court, so Magic has a great passing angle to his left or right. They are not just working hard; they are practicing with a purpose so they can play with a purpose. I get a shiver of excitement down my back as I sense what an adventure this mission is going to be. I flashback to Riley's words about working with the greatest athletes in the world.

He was right. I study Pat as he studies the team. Nothing gets by him. He is in constant tune with the team and the mission. He sets short, medium, and long term goals for everyone on the team. He stresses that for the mission to be successful, we must all be on the same page. This is not easy when you have alpha males with egos and agendas. I learn for a mission to be accomplished, you can't just want it. There are steps. One should write their goals down on paper and be specific about them. Set priorities, timelines, and refer to them often for progress.

As I prepare the team for practice with stretching and warmups the next day, I notice a big burly guy yelling something at me that doesn't exactly sound like "Welcome to the Lakers." It's the Lakers legendary broadcaster Chick Hearn, a spoken-word artist who invented much of the modern vocabulary of pro basketball: "air ball," "slam dunk," "no harm, no foul." And "Coop-a-Loop" for when Magic throws Cooper a high-arching lob that he slams down for a powerful dunk. Riley had warned me that each year Hearn liked to pick out a target among the new hires. Figuring the best defense is a good offense, I yell right back at him: "I heard about you – give me your best shot." Somehow it works to get him off my back even before he has a chance to really start in on me. From that day forward, Chick treats me like an adopted son and becomes an important mentor.

Soon Chick and I are always together. But Chick is not part of Riley's 12+2+1 formulation, and that creates a dilemma for me. It means Chick, believe it or not, is considered a peripheral opponent, someone I can't share certain information with. Like who is injured, how badly, and who may not be playing that night. It is frustrating for me, but even more frustrating for Chick. In addition to broadcasting, he had been an assistant General Manager back when Jack Kent Cooke owned the team. He thinks I should tell him what is going on in the training room. Riley doesn't want me sharing that information with anyone, so I can't. Not even with Chick. Sharing that information is detrimental to the mission.

This leads to some really awkward moments. Like when Chick learns from someone else at the last minute that a player is injured and is not going to play that night. An annoyed Chick says right on the air, "Vitti didn't tell us anything about this injury." I just have to take the on-air abuse. I'm caught in the middle between my growing friendship with Chick and my loyalty to Riley's 12+2+1 code. But other than that issue we are as tight as two men from different generations can be.

One of the Lakers' athletic trainer's many duties is to double as the traveling secretary. Everything I know about that part of the job I learn from Chick. He is always on a fast break. Always the first one on the plane and the bus. Always the first one off. He gets up at the crack of dawn. No matter how early I get up, he is always waiting for me in the hotel lobby with hot coffee and the local newspaper. He teaches me how to move a team around the country. He goes with me to the airport to show me how to check in the players, who to tip, and how much. It's not my favorite part of the job. I didn't train to become a traveling secretary I trained to become an athletic trainer but what I do realize is it puts me in charge of a lot of things, and when you are in charge you don't have to rely on other people, they have to rely on you.

I realize that being valid and reliable in whatever is asked of you becomes paramount to the success of the mission. Although the traveling secretary is not under the sports medicine umbrella, I try to perform the duties as best I can. After all who else is going to do it in the 12 + 2+ 1. The players can't, and the coaches won't - so that leaves me. It's all part of the mission, and for the mission to be successful, you may have to do things that you don't want to do. I learned when that day comes, welcome the task, and do it to the best of your ability.

CHAPTER 2

LEADERSHIP: A PHYSICAL PRESENCE BY SOMEONE THAT HAS EARNED AND COMMANDS RESPECT

Within a couple of hours of waking up on Saturday of Memorial Day weekend 1985, I have the team taken by bus to the Boston Garden for our first practice. The Garden was built in 1928. I'm sure it was something special back then. I like old things and nostalgia, but now It's an ugly, rapidly aging, badly deteriorating athletic venue that's seen much better days.

Of course, Celtics fans see it differently. For them, it's hallowed ground. It's where their beloved Celtics won 15 NBA championships. The Celtics – and their fans -- love bringing the opposing team into the Garden, (pronounced Gaahden locally) to torture them. The Garden is the Celtics sixth man, a home-court advantage unlike any other in the league. For them, a ticket to the Garden is a ticket to basketball heaven. There are plenty of seats with only a partial view because their sightlines are obstructed by support columns. But Celtic fans are still eager to pay good money to sit behind a pole - just to be part of the action. Even the clear-view seats are rusty with chipped paint flaking off them. The lower section seats are much closer to the playing floor than in other arenas around the league. When the crowd is chanting epithets or screaming curses, threats and racial slurs at the visiting players – which happens a lot in Boston -- it's like a tidal wave of sound washing over the opposing team.

The run-down conditions extend to the opposing team's bench. The seats that we sit on are old metal taupe-colored folding chairs like those you find in a high school auditorium built in the 1950s. Half of them are bent and lopsided, the worst ones they can find in the entire Garden. Naturally, the Celtics themselves have good seats.

Then there is the famous parquet floor, a geometric mosaic of wood pieces. It's filled with dead spots where the ball suddenly stops bouncing. Perhaps it's because the wood pieces allegedly came from old whiskey barrels. Of course, the Celtics know every inch of that floor by heart. The league rules allow hand-checking, so the Celtics steer opposing dribblers towards the dead spots, where they can steal the ball or cause a turnover. No opposing team, no matter how well prepared, can match that kind of detailed home court knowledge. It's like trying to maneuver through a minefield. You don't know where the mines are. But the Celtics do.

The visitor's locker room is notoriously small, freezing during the winter regular-season games and blistering hot during the NBA finals in June. The only windows are those ancient kinds of upper transom windows that are impossible to reach and can only be opened at a partial angle.

Actually, to call it a "locker" room is an unfunny joke. There are no lockers in any traditional sense. Only nails and hooks on the wall for each player to hang his street clothes on. It's hard to believe, but it's the truth: the nails are so close together that the players are on top of each other as they dress and undress with little separation and even less personal space.

The room is so narrow that when Riley does his video review and pre-game chalk talks, I have to set the VCR up so that the 7 or 8 guys in the playing rotation are in the middle of the room so they can see what's going on. The reserves are relegated to the outer fringes and can't see much of anything. And the shower room is the only place Riley and Bertka can do their pre-game prep work with the TV and VCR before meeting with the players.

Celtics President and General Manager Red Auerbach does nothing about any of these problems because he thinks it helps the Celtics win. And that's all that matters to him. There is no fairness and/or sportsmanship. Grab every advantage you can. That's his philosophy, and it filters down through the entire organization. All the way down to equipment manager Wayne Lebeaux. Over the years Wayne and I have become great friends, but in those days he wasn't beyond sticking it to you if he could, and he did it with a smile. Why do they do petty things like this? Just to annoy us and make our jobs more difficult. To distract us. So they'll have a better chance to beat us. Every little edge helps. Most teams don't do this kind of stuff because it's considered unprofessional. Others don't do it on the theory that you don't want to piss the visiting team off and give them more motivation. But for some reason, the Celtics – and especially Red – take great pleasure in doing it. I never understood that mindset. My GM, Jerry West was as competitive as anyone that walked the planet, but he had so much class that he would never stand for that type of behavior. His philosophy was much more like treat them with dignity then go out on the floor and kick their asses.

But five years later I watched the classic gangster film Good-fellas, and I understood a little better. In a scene where Joe Pesci and Robert DeNiro are having a late-night dinner at Pesci's mother's house – with a dead body in their car's trunk -- they talk about a funny-looking guy in a painting on the kitchen wall. Pesci uses an old Italian phrase – "conuto contente" to describe the guy. Now, my father and all of my grandparents were born in Italy, but I had never heard that phrase and didn't understand it. Then Pesci explained it, and I immediately thought of Red Auerbach: "It means he's content to be a jerk...and doesn't care who knows it." That was Red in a nutshell: happy to be a jerk and proud of it.

On top of all the other problems Red won't fix, the Garden has no air conditioning. That, Riley felt, was a critical factor in a couple of the losses during the 1984 Finals. In one game, the temperature inside our locker room reached 105 degrees. Courtside it was 97 degrees, and 36-year-old Kareem Abdul-Jabbar had to gulp pure oxygen just to keep playing.

When I arrived at the Forum on my first day on the job, I found all these little electric fans stuck back in a storage room. I asked around and learned it was the only thing they could think of to fight the heat and humidity in the Garden locker room during the '84 Finals. It didn't do much good, but still, they were saving the fans in case they played the Celtics again in the Finals. I thought to myself: we can do better than this. If we get back to the Garden for a Finals re-match, I'll find something better. That fall, while at a New York Giants-Oakland Raiders football game at the LA Coliseum, I noticed the Raiders players gathering around two huge air conditioning units on the sideline. On the side of each, it said MovinCool. I made a mental note to call this MovinCool company if we played the Celtics again in the Finals.

So once I know we are going to play Boston I call George Anderson, head athletic trainer for the Raiders, to get a contact for MovinCool. The company president says he is a big Lakers fan. In exchange for two tickets to the Finals, he agrees to send two of the air conditioning units to our locker room at the Garden.

****

The Celtics finish their practice, and we take the floor. A few minutes later, Riley, always an intense guy but now wired as tight as I've ever seen him, notices a jug of Gatorade. Traditionally, the home team supplies visitors with ice, towels, and Gatorade. But as soon as he sees the Gatorade, he becomes suspicious.

PR: Gary, who put that there? Is it ours? Or did the Celtics leave it for us?
GV: The Celtics.
PR: Get rid of it - They might have spiked it with something.

It sounds crazy paranoid to me, but I get rid of it anyway. We have our own sports drink, a product called Pripps that I got from the Swedish cycling team. We even have individual cups that we keep hermetically sealed. We are leaving nothing to

23

chance. It's a hard practice, with the entire group – 12 players, two coaches, and me – focused on preparing for the day of redemption we all feel is right around the corner. From day one of the season, I did not doubt that this year, we would get our revenge on the Celtics. That feeling is only growing stronger. An hour into the practice, Riley spots someone way up in the rafters, near the ceiling. It appears to be someone looking down at our practice. Riley turns to me again. Gary, get someone up there to check it out. It could be someone spying on our practice. He's holding something. It could be a camera.

So I send our PR guy, Josh Rosenfeld, up to check it out. Turns out to be a janitor sleeping on the job while holding a mop. Rosenfeld tells him he has to leave. I report this back to Riley. He tells me to keep a sharp eye out for spies.

Rosenfeld now gives Riley, whom we usually call Riles, a new nickname: Norman Bates, from the paranoid killer in Alfred Hitchcock's "Psycho." I think it's a little over the top but in my mind who knows better than Pat. Over time, as he ratchets up his us-against-the-world intensity, his perfectionism and his fanatical devotion to controlling every detail of Lakers' life, the nickname sticks among Lakers players and front office types who whisper it among themselves. I also think to myself that maybe I have a bit of Norman Bates in me because I get where he's coming from.

The next day, Sunday is more of the same. Long, hard practices. A grim determined Riley. A focused group of players confident that they have done the extra work to ensure we will win this time. Finally, it's Monday, Memorial Day. Gameday. Right on schedule, the MovinCool company truck pulls up outside our locker room a couple of hours before the game. The two units are dragged into our locker room. They barely fit. When I plug them in, it immediately blows out half the Garden's antiquated electrical system. Our locker room goes dark. A Garden operations guy shows up and complains. My attitude was

24

to let them complain. What are they going to do – throw us out of the arena? They reboot the electrical system - I plug the MovinCool units back in.

Riley repeatedly makes it clear to everyone that we are not to allow the Celtics to take advantage of us in any way. So, I am just doing my job of standing up to their abuse.

Before the game, Riley reminds the players that there will be a $500 fine for anyone who allows an uncontested layup. And a $500 fine for anyone who helps a Celtic player up off the floor. This all stems from a turning-point incident during the 1984 Finals. In the third quarter of Game 4 of the '84 Finals, the Lakers were playing free, fast and easy.

We were cruising to a victory that would have put us up 3-1. Halfway through the third quarter our gritty, hardworking power forward Kurt Rambis was about to end a typical Showtime fast break – a long outlet pass from Abdul-Jabbar to a streaking Worthy, who quickly found a driving Rambis -- with an emphatic dunk. But Celtics power forward Kevin McHale, yet another All-Star in a Finals full of All-Stars, took him down with a clothesline tackle that drove Rambis to the floor, head-first that could have broken his neck. That was the part of the play that the media focused on.

They said it took us out of our speed and quickness game to the point where we started trying to play the Celtics style: a bully-boy brute force game we used to call goon ball. That was partly true. But the part of the play we focused on came right after Rambis went down. He leaped to his feet, spun and charged McHale, intent on payback. But Worthy, a fundamentally decent man who learned sportsmanship under Coach Dean Smith at North Carolina, stepped between them. He accidentally knocked Rambis back over a courtside cameraman and into the crowd. Worthy's action defused the situation, but the play changed the tone of the game. It showed the Lakers just how far the Celtics were willing to go to win. By today's rules, it would have been a flagrant two foul. McHale would have been booted from the game and suspended. The Lakers would have gotten two shots plus the ball. The way the NBA game was played in 1984, McHale was hit with only a technical foul, one free throw and he was able to continue to play. In the Celtics' view – and many in the media agreed -- we were the soft guys that prevented our fallen teammate from fighting back. The Celtics won that game in overtime and turned the series around. To make matters worse, all this happened on our home court in front of our adoring fans - right in front of Jack Nicholson and Dyan Cannon.

It must have looked like a horror movie to them.

The rest of the 1984 Finals was fought on their terms – a down and dirty brawl. Worthy later admitted to me that he regretted stepping between Rambis and McHale. He had acted on a good instinct – sportsmanship. But that only works if both teams are practicing it. We thought it was a knife fight. The Celtics came with guns loaded for bear. They won.

****

So now, a year later, Riley lays down new rules to ensure that this time we won't act soft but the internal doubts are still there. Are we tough enough to stand up to the Boston bullies? Are we weak men used to a beachy lifestyle? Glamour queens from Hollywood who don't have the guts, the desire, the determination to do what it take to win at crunch time?

All this self-doubting psycho-drama is swirling in the background as we prepare for game one of the re-match. It sure feels like we are emotionally, spiritually, and physically ready for the battle ahead. Now we will have to prove it in what is sure to be a down-to-the-wire first game as both teams struggle to establish dominance.The Celtics win the opening tip-off. McHale, the thug who leveled Rambis a year ago, hits a bunch of buckets early for a quick lead. Riley calls a timeout. It does no good as the Celtics keep on scoring and we keep on missing. Riley calls another time out. But we can't stop the bleeding.

The players are in shock. They're unable to respond to Riley's instructions, to his pleas for more energy. Kareem, in particular, looks like he is running in mud while the Celtics are flowing up and down the court. Towards the end of the first quarter, guard Danny Ainge, hits a short jumper. Then another jumper. Then a driving layup. Then three more jumpers to give him six straight baskets. Before we know what hit us, they are up 38-24 at the end of the first quarter. Unbelievably, it feels like it's already over. And it is definitely over at halftime when they go into their locker room with a 79-49 lead. The Garden crowd howls with joy and laughs mockingly at our ineptitude. The shock and pain are unbearable. It feels like someone died.

Like we died.

The players are comatose in the locker room. Even preacher-man Riley can't make us believe we have a chance to come back from a 30-point deficit. The worst part is knowing we have to sit through another half in this torture chamber. Our fans at home can turn off the TV when it gets too painful. We have no choice but to sit there and absorb the pain, the abuse, and the humiliation. We can't overcome the 30-point deficit, and it ends with a surreal 148-114 final score. We are all in shock. We expected anything – a big win, a close loss – except this: a Celtics blowout of record proportions. The smart guys in the media can't wait to put a label on it: The Memorial Day Massacre. A Celtics reserve named Scott Wedman hit all 11 of his shots – including four three-pointers – to lead the Celtics with 26 points, matching McHale's total. Somebody should have hit Wedman with a hard foul after his third or fourth bucket. But nobody did. Worthy leads us with 20 points, followed by Magic with 19. Kareem has a measly 12 points and just three rebounds. Celtics center Robert Parish beat him down the floor so often it was painful, like watching an older man trying to race a young buck.

I don't say it out loud, but suddenly, I begin to lose my faith in the mission. I gave up my life's mission to buy into the Lakers' mission, and this is payback? The Celtics were so superior it is hard to picture any way we can win four out of the next six games. It might not even go seven games. I can see them winning four straight or three out of the next four to close out the series. Losing by 34 points after all our preparation and planning will do that to you.

The locker room is like a morgue. Even Magic and Riley, the two most vocal members of the 12+2+1 tribe, are silent. Finally, Kareem, the least vocal of the group, the most solitary man on the team, clears his throat to speak. With his still-wet jersey clinging to his 7-foot-2 wiry-strong frame and his trademark goggles pushed to the top of his head, he starts speaking slowly. I want to apologize to all of you - I had migraines, and I played like garbage - but I won't play like that anymore. We're going to win this thing. He takes a long pause and repeats himself. I promise. We are going to win this thing.

I realize I am watching greatness in action. Not the run-jump-and-shoot kind of greatness that fans cheer on the court and the media celebrate in print and with video highlights. The kind of off-court greatness involving responsibility, accountability, and quiet leadership that the fans and the media don't get to see. I feel privileged to be in the room.

Kareem's words are encouraging. This was when I learned you could tell a lot about the character of a person when things are going bad, not when it's all going your way. Kareem taught me that day that when things go wrong, you look in the mirror and start with that person. The next stage is to beat yourself up over it. It's part of the process, but it's not very productive. The sooner you get through that stage, the better. The most important part is to learn from your mistakes and do not repeat them. The message is clear to me. The fool is the one that never learns from their mistakes and continues to repeat them. The wise person is the one that does learn from their mistakes and never makes the same mistake twice. The prudent person not only learns from their own mistakes but learns from the mistakes of others. Try to be prudent, always be wise, never be the fool. My faith in the mission is restored.

But Riley is still grimmer – and more determined -- than I have ever seen him. The bus trip back to the Marriott is a zombie ride. Dinner is silence broken only by low murmurings of disbelief and shock. Riley tells everyone to get to bed early because we are going back to work tomorrow morning. We have three full days before the next game on Thursday night. It will be the three most important days in Lakers history. Three defining days. For all of us: 12 players, two coaches, and me.

****

The first order of business Tuesday morning is a video review session of the first game. It's held in a hotel conference room. Kareem usually sits in the back row. Today he comes in and plants himself in the front row. He knows for the whole team, but for himself, especially, it will be a horror show.

Riley holds nothing back. Every time Parish beats Kareem down the court, Riley runs it over and over. He points out how Kareem is letting down his teammates. How his breakdowns are leading to team breakdowns. How Celtics backup big man Greg Kite, a thuggish, borderline NBA player with minimal skills, had continued the beat down Parish put on him. Kareem just sits there and doesn't say a word. No excuses. But it's not just Kareem. Riley calls out Magic, Coop, and Scott, who like to think of themselves as the three musketeers. The Celtics guard trio of Dennis Johnson, Ainge and Wedman just destroyed them and the whole world was watching. Riley goes right down the roster. He is taking aim at everyone who played. No one is spared. It feels like no one will get out of this room alive. But eventually, they do slink out. Heads down. Eyes dead to the outside world.

At practice, Kareem breaks another long-standing tradition. All season long Riley has excused him from most practices, so he can save himself for the games. The other players and Riley encourage Kareem to sit out these practices too. But he insists on participating in everything for the next three days. He does every drill, every sprint, every everything. He is leading by example. After the video session, no one says a word. These proud men, this band of brothers, act as champions and focus on the mission. They keep their heads down, work hard, and do whatever Riley says to do. There's only one way back, and that's to win the game Thursday night.

And then win the series.

I'm doing all my usual things with the players: stretching, therapy, weight training. And I'm watching how they're handling the disaster that was game one. I'm starting to reach a strange conclusion: it might have been better for us to lose by 34 points than by one or two. I've always believed that you learn more from losing than from winning. It forces you to look in the mirror and admit your weaknesses. And this is such a monumental loss that the players are unusually open to learning what they need to do differently, what they need to change to get a different result. This way there's no lucky Celtic shot to blame. No bad call by the officials to blame. No unexpected Lakers' injury to blame. The shock, pain, and humiliation are so great that it rips the scab off any possible excuses or rationalizations. Now it's clear to the players and the rest of us that we will have to confront our demons and figure out why we can't beat the Celtics. They are a great team, but we are a better team. We just have to prove it, and we better start proving it Thursday night or this whole Finals will quickly be over.

Thursday comes around at last. As we board the bus to go to the Garden, I see something I never thought I would see: Kareem has his father with him as he boards the bus. Kareem knows Riley's hard and fast rule: no one outside the 12+2+1 is to ride on the team bus. Ever. And the rule has never been violated. Ever.

But this time I watch in shock – the whole team watches in shock – as Riley sticks his hand out and silently welcomes Ferdinand Lewis Alcindor Sr. onto the bus. No words are exchanged as they shake hands. Riley is intuitive enough to understand what is happening. Kareem needs a little help confronting his inner demons. Riley knows who this tall, distinguished-looking gentleman is without being told. We all know who he is. We know that Kareem's father was a metro cop in New York City. We've all heard Kareem's stories about how his father chased an armed criminal into a subway tunnel and onto the train tracks. That takes courage. So there's a certain measure of pre-cooked respect involved when he walks onto the bus. Still, it's an extraordinary sight. Riley's reaction is extraordinary. As I watch this encounter, it somehow feels precisely right and fitting for this most crucial moment in Lakers' history. It feels like the fate of the franchise is a passenger on the bus. If we can't complete the mission of beating the Celtics, we'll always be second-best. We ride to the Garden with complete and total silence on the bus.

As the silence becomes louder and louder, I realize I am witnessing part of Riley's greatness. Even the most rigid and demanding leader must show flexibility and human compassion at certain rare times. This is one of those times. If Kareem needs his father at his side to perform at his best in the biggest game of his life, then he will be allowed to have his father by his side. For this single time, 12+2+1 will be 12+2+1+1 because that is what is best for the team at this moment. And that is all that matters: what is best for the team. Riley is inspired to ditch his pre-game prepared talk. Those talks are usually pretty good. Riley is a natural-born motivational speaker who puts significant time into preparing his talks. He makes notes and everything. But this spontaneous talk, inspired by the surprise appearance of Kareem's father, is unique. This time he starts talking about his own father, Leon Francis Riley. A minor-league baseball player who played a few games in the majors but never achieved his dreams. He tells us how, as a kid, his father made his older brothers bring Pat to the park with them. How every day Pat would get beat up. One day he was even chased home by a boy with a butcher knife. Finally, his brothers asked his father why he made them take Pat with them. His father explained that he wanted Pat to learn not to be afraid. That there comes a time in everyone's life when you have to plant your feet, take a stand and kick some ass.

He describes his last exchange with his father. It was at his wedding reception back in June 1970. His father was leaving the reception in the back seat of a car driven by one of Pat's brothers. As Pat jogged alongside the car to say goodbye, his father leaned out the window and reminded him of what he had been telling him since he was 12 years old. Just remember what I always taught you. Somewhere, someplace, sometime, you're going to have to plant your feet, make a stand, and kick some ass. And when that time comes, you do it.

His father died a couple of months later. Who knows if it's a true story? I assume it is. But it doesn't really matter. Because it works.

The team is so fired up they're ready to run through a brick wall for Pat. After three days spent breaking them down with stony silence, harsh criticism and blatant contempt, in ten electric minutes, Riley has built them back up to an emotional peak. This was when I learned another valuable lesson: that leadership starts with someone that has earned and commands respect. They don't have to do or say anything – just their appearance says it all. And that is what Kareem's father

32

was to us that day: an inspiration. Riley's story about his own father was directly inspired by Kareem's father showing up to ride the bus with us.

The game starts, and no one plays better than Kareem. He's throwing in sky hooks from everywhere and nailing them both left-handed and right-handed. A true artist was showing off his incredible skills and making his father proud. But it's the way he's doing it that is so striking. Gone is the phlegmatic, low-key Kareem who keeps his emotions hidden behind his huge insect-eye goggles. The bench players are jumping up and pointing at him every time he scores. He screams back at them: "See, I told you! Yeah! Yeah!!"

None of us have ever seen him like this before. We've seen him get mad once in a while, like the time he squared off with Larry Bird during the '84 Finals. But that was him losing his cool and hurting his team. This is something completely differ-ent: Kareem allowing his inner competitor to come out for the world to see. This is Kareem smiling, sweating, luxuriating in his talent, his hard work and his bond with his teammates and his audience.

He finishes with 30 points, 17 rebounds, 8 assists, and 3 blocks. He demolishes Parish, an All-Star in his own right. Greg Kite? A mosquito that Kareem swats away with one sky-hook after another. Of course, Kareem doesn't do it alone. Coop hits eight out of nine shots for 22 points and plays lock-down D on Bird. Magic is orchestrating the fast break as well as I've ever seen him. It's not like the Celtics roll over for us. They are a great team. Defending champions. They know how important this game is. If they win it, they're heavy favor-ites to repeat as champs. They fight to the final buzzer, but we prevail 109-102. It stands alone, then and now, as the most important victory in Laker history. We have confronted our in-ner demons. We have planted our feet and taken a stand. And it feels so good. Too good for some of us. Josh Rosenfeld, the

33

short, pudgy PR guy, can't control his overflowing emotions.

After the game, he brings Kareem courtside for an interview. As Kareem waits for the production crew to set up, a cluster of Boston fans starts taunting him with chants of "Lew! Lew!" He was born Lewis Alcindor Jr. but changed it to Kareem Abdul-Jabbar when he became a Muslim. Their taunts are ugly, mean, and could be considered racist.

As Kareem starts to boil over, Rosenfeld hurls a wet towel at the group of fans. It smacks Parish's wife Nancy right in the face. Next thing I know, M.L. Carr rushes into our locker room, acting all pissed off and demanding some apology. I wonder why Carr is in our locker room, but Parish isn't.

Riley is pissed off too. He knows this single off-court moment could easily blow up into one of his dreaded peripheral opponents. Something the Celtics can rally around. He demands Rosenfeld do something to defuse the crisis before Game 3, which will be Sunday back in LA at the Forum. I can't help wondering if Red Auerbach would have had the same reaction. He probably would have congratulated Rosenfeld for throwing the towel. Rosenfeld, the skilled communicator that he is, writes Parish an abject letter of apology that he plans to leave in the Celtics locker room before the game. But when he spots Parish walking into the Forum before game 3, he walks up to him and asks for a minute of his time. He tells him how awful he feels. How he had no idea, it was Parish's wife in the group of fans, how it's the lowest point of his career.

Parish is nicknamed Chief after the tall, silent crazy guy in the great Ken Kesey novel – and equally great Jack Nicholson film -- One Flew Over the Cuckoo's Nest. He stares down at him and says nothing in response. Finally, a desperate Rosenfeld, more than a foot shorter than the 6-foot-11 Parish, looks up at him. "Are you mad at me?" Parish smiles down at him. "Hell no. I've been telling her to keep her mouth shut for ten years. You're the first guy to get her to finally do it." They shake hands, and the towel-in-the-face crisis is over.

****

Now there's a game to be played with the series tied 1-1. In theory, this is still an even series that could go either way, but we have now gained the advantage. Game two was a turning point not just in this series, but in Lakers' history. We have broken the Celtics curse over us. Now we have the psychological edge, and we're not going to let it go. We dominate game 3 to go up 2-1 with a 136-111 wipeout. Boston fights back in Game 4 when a double-teamed Bird passes to an open Dennis Johnson, who hits an 18-foot jumper at the buzzer for a 107-105 win. The press is buzzing about this being an all-time classic series, even better than the '84 Finals. Celtics Coach K.C. Jones compares the series to the recent middleweight slugfest between Marvin Hagler and Tommy "Hit Man" Hearns. We made the smart play when we double-teamed Bird at the end of Game 4. He is a much better shooter than Johnson. But Johnson, a great defender who always plays better in the clutch, hit the shot for the win. That will happen with great players. But to us, it doesn't signal any fundamental change in the dynamics at play here. We are the better team. We know it. The Celtics know it. We proved it in Game 2 when we absolutely had to win. And we'll prove it again in the next game. Besides, under the NBA's new 2-3-2 home game format for the Finals, game 5 will again be played in the Forum, where there's no way we are going to lose such a pivotal game.

This time the heroes are the power forwards Rambis and his backup, Mitch Kupchak, who used to be an All-Star caliber player but now has been reduced to a substitute because of a devastating knee injury. They are both so physical in game 5 that Celtic announcer Johnny Most compares them to rats that crawled out of the sewer. The name-calling doesn't bother us as we grab a 120-111 win in front of our delirious fans.

Jack Nicholson is in his usual courtside seat mugging for the crowd and the cameras. A local showoff named Dancing Barry, sporting sunglasses and a purple-and-gold tuxedo whips the crowd into a frenzy. The Laker Girls let it all hang out.

Now we head back to Boston with a 3-2 lead and an unprecedented opportunity: to win an NBA championship on the Celtics parquet floor. The Lakers have never done that. Actually, no NBA team has ever done that. Now we have two shots at it: games 6 and 7 will both be played in the Garden. A game 6 win is all we need, and indeed that's what we do to finally complete the mission.

Kareem scores 29 points, and Worthy adds 27 to lead us to a 111-100 victory. Kareem is quickly named the Finals MVP, and it is well deserved. He kept the promise he made to his teammates after Game 1. He is the MVP, but an assist should go to his father and Riley for allowing his father on the bus. That decision taught me that leadership starts from a physical presence by someone at the top that has earned and commands respect.

The old cramped locker room that we all despise becomes the scene of the greatest, most joyful celebration I have ever been a part of. We spray champagne on each other till the floor is a wide Sargasso Sea of alcohol. We hug till it feels like we're going to suffocate each other.

We know in our hearts that it's mission accomplished, and it will never get better than that.

CHAPTER 3

IF YOU DON'T LIKE WHERE YOU ARE, HAVE THE COURAGE AND WORK ETHIC TO CHANGE IT

People ask me often, how did you become the head athletic trainer for the Los Angeles Lakers. Well, anyone that knows me knows that I make short stories long and long stories longer, so here's my story.

Whether it's basketball or just life in general, I never wanted to be a whiner. It's a product of the intense work ethic I inherited from my beloved father Mario, who worked all day almost every day – for more than 55 years -- in a factory making lady's handbags. God bless him and his ferocious work ethic. It's the true-north foundation of all the good things that have happened in my life and in my sibling's lives. His attitude was to put your head down and work. The world is a hard place, you try to make a better life than you had for your children, and then you die.

My philosophy was a bit different. If you didn't like your situation, whining about it wasn't going to help, staying in the situation was not an option, so if you're not happy, do something about it. I'm a creature of habit once I find what I like, but I'm not afraid of change, and that's precisely what I did when I realized my first career choice, meteorology wasn't going the way I wanted it to.

It was summer 1979, three years after I had graduated from Southern Connecticut State University with a degree in speech communications and absolutely no idea what I wanted to do with the rest of my life. I spent my first three post-college years trying blue-collar factory jobs that led to a three-piece suit and some wing-tip shoes for a white-collar salesman job that left me without a true sense of purpose; other than making money. So with the aid of my ever-helpful sister Carol, I did some research and decided to study meteorology because I had always been good at science and I liked nature and the outdoors. It seemed like a good idea at the time.

After spending my entire life on the east coast – I was born and raised in Connecticut and was living in New York City at the time -- I left everything behind. Against the advice of friends and family, I split for the University of Utah to study meteorology. Almost immediately, I began to suspect I had made a big mistake. The curriculum was physics on top of math on top of physics on top of math. I don't remember much about those classes other than the sine, cosine, and vectors.

I quickly realized I was in a classroom full of brainiacs, and I wasn't going to be the Kobe Bryant of physics. Oh, I was smart enough and could do the work alright, but it didn't come nearly as quickly to me as it did to others in the same program. It didn't feel like a natural fit. There was no passion in it for me, just drudgery that wore me down.

The fall semester dragged on until Christmas break finally arrived just in time. I was at my breaking point and needed someone to vent to. Telling my family about my problem was out of the question. They had urged me not to go west in the first place. There was no way I could crawl home with my tail between my legs.

Luckily my two college buddies, Rich Corso, and Richard "Doc" Ludeman were living in Los Angeles. They had both been competitive swimmers during our time at Southern Connecticut State, and now they were on the coaching staff at UCLA. Corso eventually went on to be a well-known USA Olympic water polo coach.

So I drove out to LA and stayed a few days with them before we all flew back east to see our families for the holidays. It was supposed to be a fun visit, but I couldn't help myself: I pissed and moaned about how I had made the wrong decision to go into meteorology. I wasn't afraid to pull the plug and do something else, I just didn't know what.

As we headed to LAX for our flight home Rich and Doc surprised me with an early Christmas present: The Sports Medicine Book, by sports science pioneer Gabe Mirkin. They weren't subtle about their intent: they said this is what you should do with your life. 40 years later, it was one of the most important gifts I ever received. In fact, I still have it and keep it in a place of honor on my bookshelf.

By the time we reached JFK airport five hours later, the entire book had been absorbed. My soul was touched, my brain was on fire, and my journey was about to veer off in a radical new direction: from meteorology to sports medicine.
.
After all these years later, it's time to say it again: thank you Doc and Rich.

****

That I should end up working in professional sports was not surprising, since I grew up in the sports-crazy town of Stamford, Connecticut. That I should end up working in professional sports was, however, also very unlikely, since I grew up in a non-sports family. I was born and raised in historic Stamford, Connecticut named after Stamford, Lincolnshire, England in 1640. The street I first lived on, Silver Hill Lane, was just a short walk from Rippowam High School. Rippowam is what the native Americans called Stamford.

The famous baseball player and manager Bobby Valentine starred in football and baseball at Rippowam High School, which sadly no longer exists. Stamford had a rich history in football, baseball, and basketball. Located just 40 miles from Manhattan, it was a metropolitan New York bedroom suburb for many pro athletes -- home to Jackie Robinson of the Brooklyn Dodgers, New York Giants football Hall of Famer Andy Robustelli and NBA commissioner J. Walter Kennedy.

As a kid, we were all acutely aware of how important sports were to our town. All us young boys wanted to be a part of that proud sports tradition. Baseball ruled in Stamford -- they even won the little league world series in 1951. But there was also Pop Warner football and CYO. (catholic youth organization) basketball available.

I was pretty good in all three of those sports at that grade-school entry-level, even making a few all-star teams and getting my name in the paper a few times. Believe me, there is no greater thrill for a pre-teen boy than seeing your name in black and white, back in the pre-internet days when everyone read the local newspaper right down to the sports briefs. Although my parents never attended any of my games, they still have some of the sports clippings from the Stamford Advocate.

When I entered Stamford Catholic High School the competition suddenly got a lot better and my budding career as a sports stud quickly came to a grinding halt. I was too small to make the football team and was the last cut for the baseball team. But I did make the junior varsity basketball squad. My friend from grammar school, Doug Smith and I were the last two to make the team. I vividly remember the coach informing us that there weren't enough uniforms for both of us. Which one of us wanted the last uniform, he asked? I was shy about it and thought maybe we could share the uniform by alternating games, but before I could make that suggestion, Doug said he would take it, and that was that. You snooze you lose, and I snoozed.

So I sat at the end of the bench with a completely different uniform than the rest of the team. In retrospect, I should have been happy to make the team, but instead, I was embarrassed and imagined everyone was staring and laughing at me. In an age of conformity, I stood out for all the wrong reasons. Then my situation went from bad to worse. I'm not sure what happened or why the atmosphere around the team changed, but the coach soon took a distinct dislike to me and naturally, the negative feelings quickly became mutual. I have a very clear memory of being at practice one day and going for a drink from the water fountain when suddenly I heard him yelling at me and ordering me to run laps. I had to keep running around the gym while he chased me and whipped the back of my legs with the lanyard that held his whistle. He also stood at half court and threw basketballs at my feet as I ran by him.

Today that kind of behavior would generate a coach's suspension and maybe even a lawsuit from a helicopter parent but back then it was standard operating procedure. It was obvious to me that he disliked me and was trying to run me off the team. The team was not very good, and we usually lost by 30 or 40 points. Near the end of those blowouts was my only chance at actually getting to play for a few mop-up minutes but even then I rarely got in the game.

My stubbornness and work ethic kicked in, and I refused to quit. I told myself to make it to the end of the season and then I would never have to play organized sports again. That's exactly what happened. I finished the season, and soon after that, I used my free time working a part-time job in the US post office.

****

At home, sports were my passion alone. My parents didn't know the difference between Mickey Mantle and Mickey Mouse. They were too busy trying to raise three children with old country Italian roman catholic values while at the same time assimilating into American culture. I often felt when walking out the front door of our home I was entering America, but when I returned home I walked into old school Italy. It was a dichotomy of cultures for me back then. Multiculturalism seems to have come a long way since I was a kid.

My father Mario emigrated from a small Italian village called Settefrati in 1937. He was 16 years old, the age when young boys were conscripted into the dictator Benito Mussolini's

Avantguardista. Just like Adolf Hitler did with the Hitler youth, Mussolini was trying to turn Italian children into fascists. My father's parents wanted no part of that, and World War II was looming on the horizon, so they shipped their only son off to America.

My grandfather Angelo Vitti and three of his daughters were already in the United States working as manual laborers and sending money back to the old country. My grandmother, Adolorata Terenzio, remained in Settefrati with my father's youngest sister. In those days women like my grandmother were referred to as white widows: women who had a husband and a marriage that was alive but they were forced to live apart for economic reasons.

I now own the home my grandmother stayed back in Italy for. I visit it every summer with my wife Martha. When friends ask about my fancy "villa" in Italy, I respond that if my family had a villa, they would not have immigrated to the United States. It was closer to a barn than a villa. My father wanted to name me Angelo after my grandfather but my mother, Sylvia, objected. She thought we should assimilate and that Angelo was too Italian of a name at a time when there was still a wide-spread prejudice against Italians. It wasn't uncommon to be called a greaseball or a wop in those days.

According to the Vitti family legend, my grandfather Angelo was nicknamed Gary because of his striking resemblance to Giuseppe Garibaldi, a famous general responsible for the unification of Italy. So, although I wasn't formally named after a saint or my grandfather I was still named after a famous Italian, because of my mother's intervention.

My father's amazing story – he passed in 2018 at 97 years of age - is a classic immigrant narrative. He landed at Ellis Island crossing the Atlantic by ship with his sister, Antonietta, who was a couple of years older. They joined the rest of the

43

family in the New York metropolitan area to work and build a better life. Grandpop was a ditch digger, a term used for a common laborer at the time, but it was honest work. My father once described the career options for a child growing up in Settefrati as:

Become an opera singer: The arts and opera were to Settefrati what sports and baseball was to
Stamford, the preferred choice.

Become a tailor: It was indoors, warm, and clean.

Become a shoemaker: Not as clean or delicate. It was harder work than a tailor but still warm and indoors.

Become a stone cutter: It was outdoors in the elements and harder work than the first three choices but it was skilled labor and paid better.

Become a ditch digger: this was my grandfather. He had no education and no marketable skill, which made him a peasant. All that was left for him was to become a ditch digger, a common laborer.

Like many countries in the mid-1930s, Italy was caught up in the great depression. There really was no work in Italy, so his choice was to seek a hard day's work in America for an honest day's wage. At 16 years old my dad was pulled out of school and put to work for a lady's handbag manufacturer, the Henry Meyers Company. He continued factory work until he was 72 years old. He provided a good life for my mother and my two sisters and me, but we never saw him.

He would leave for work in the morning when it was dark and came home after work when it was dark. I believe the worst day of his life is the day he retired because that was all he knew how to do -- and that's all that we knew about him.

Sports did not exist for my father and my mother. There was no playing ball in the yard, no watching games on tv together, no going to the park for pick-up games. When I had a little league game, I rode my bicycle there and back alone, it was never a family event. Twice a year our family went instead to the opera, to a symphony or to a broadway show because both mom and dad loved the arts.

Only once did we attend a sporting event together. I remember going to the "old-old" Yankee stadium in 1959 when I was 5 years old. I say the "old-old" Yankee stadium because it was the one before the one they now call the old Yankee stadium. I'm talking three stadiums ago, it was the house that Babe Ruth built back in 1923.

I remember how the grass seemed neon-bright green, and the famous monuments in center field were in fair territory. I saw Mickey Mantle, and Roger Maris play, and I have home movies to prove it. I think my dad got the tickets from his boss but beyond that one Yankees game sports was simply not on the radar in our home.

So a career in sports never crossed my mind. My father's dream was for me to be a dentist. I never quite understood why he would want his son working in other people's mouths all day. It might have been his dream, but it certainly wasn't mine.

As a Vitti, all we knew was hard work. The factory where dad worked would close for two weeks in the summer over the 4th of July. That's when we went on our annual two-day family vacation. My dad loved president John F. Kennedy, so we would go to Hyannis Port on Cape Cod near where the Kennedy compound was. We could only afford to go for a weekend staying at the Presidential Motor Lodge. Instead of numbers, the motel rooms had the names of presidents. Although pop loved Kennedy, my mom loved Ike, so we always asked for the Eisenhower room. There were double beds, mom and dad in one, my two sisters in the other and me on the roll away in front of the door. If you wanted out of the room, you had to go through me.

After our vacation weekend, pop spent the rest of his vacation painting the outside of the house. I was his right-hand man, hauling the ladder, cleaning the brushes and moving the drip tarp. His work ethic was imprinted on me by his example. He not only preached hard work – he did it both at the factory and around the house. He was always busy, so I learned early on how to make a buck with hard work. I washed cars, cut grass, weeded, shoveled snow, and even had a shoeshine box. But all those odd jobs were just a warm-up for what was coming.

The first day after school ended for the summer between 8th grade and freshman year in high school, my father woke me up at the crack of dawn. He hadn't warned me the night before, so I thought the school year was over and I was free for the summer, but pop didn't see it that way. He put me in the car and drove me to Woodway Country Club in nearby Darien. He brought me to the caddy shack that had an Italian caddy master, introduced me and asked him to put me to work. I was too small to carry the big leather golf bags popular back then, so instead, I cleaned shoes, clubs, and golf balls for a few 25 cent tips here and there.

The next year, however, I was able to carry a bag 18 holes for $2.00 a round. After working all day at the caddy shack, there was a 5-mile walk home. I never thought there was anything wrong or strange about this. It was normal for me, and I always left the club happy because I had a couple of dollars in my pocket.

****

Back to the book that changed my life. It's amazing the difference one single book can make on a person's life and career. As I said earlier, I returned to the University of Utah after the

46

1979 holiday break feeling like I had found my calling thanks to my friend's early Christmas gift of The Sports Medicine Book by Gabe Mirkin. I made a beeline to the training room and asked to meet with Bill Bean, the head athletic trainer. Bill was unbelievably cordial and professional. He gave me his valuable time and listened to my situation. He shared his feelings and passion about his profession but told me it was impossible to get into his program. There was no space for me. They only allowed so many students in the major, and there were no vacancies. Once again, my work ethic kicked into overdrive.

I asked if I could come around during my free time and be a fly on the wall. I promised I would not talk to anyone or touch anything. I just wanted to observe to make sure this is what I wanted to do for the rest of my life. If the answer was yes, then I would find a program at some other school.

Meanwhile, I continued to go to classes in the meteorology program, I bartended at night and in between I was in the training room. It's an interesting phenomenon: if you hang around a place long enough you begin to become a part of it's fabric. Anyone that has been in a division I college football training room knows how crazy it can be. These guys are big, aggressive and there's a lot of testosterone floating around in the air. After a few weeks of observation, there came a day when I was in my corner, and a football player asked for something. I don't remember what it was, but it was something benign like a band-aid. I didn't want to overstep my bounds, but I wanted to help, and I knew I could. I went over to Bill and said hey Bill that big guy over there asked me to get him something and I know where it is, should I do it? He was so busy he said yeah, sure, do it. With that simple act, I had crossed the line between thinking about sports medicine and actually participating in it. Not long after there was a huge snowfall up in the ski areas and some of the student athletic trainers called in sick for their shifts so they could go skiing. Bill was no dummy

47

as he knew what they did and he kicked them out of the program for blowing off their shifts -- which made room for me. He told me I was more dedicated as an observer than some of them were as full time matriculated students. He promised he would find a spot for me and he did.

I worked for the rest of the year for that opportunity. I switched out of the meteorology program and into the athletic training program. I began by taking anatomy and physiology and entrenched myself in my new education. I spent every moment I could in the medical library learning about the human body. I quickly completed the undergraduate core curriculum for athletic training and then received a graduate assistantship to enter the master's degree program.

I put myself in the right place at the right time. I found myself and what I wanted to do with my life and I didn't just want to be good at it, I wanted to be the best. Bill Bean saw that drive in me and gave me a chance, and for that alone, I am forever in his debt. I completed my master's degree and started my Ph.D. in 1982. In those days, NBA teams did not have practice sites so they would rent court time where ever they could find a decent gym.

The Portland Trailblazers practiced at the University of Portland. Their basketball program had just gained national attention with Darwin Cook and Jose Slaughter getting drafted into the NBA. Portland athletics was looking to hire an athletic trainer, but they wanted to integrate that hire with the department of education to begin an athletic training curriculum. Athletic director Joe Etzel asked the head athletic trainer for the Blazers, Ron Culp if he knew of someone that might fit what they were looking for. Ron knew me through my affiliation with the Jazz and knew I was working on my Ph.D., so he recommended me and off I went to the pacific northwest to build my own program. I continued to work on my degree in absentia while writing the athletic training curriculum as well as designing a state of the art training room, weight room, and human performance lab. My basketball network was beginning to expand. I was a football and baseball athletic trainer at the University of Utah but they had a rich basketball tradition. While I was there Tom Chambers, Danny Vranes and Pace Mannion were on the team -- all of them future NBA draftees.

My affiliation with the Utah Jazz began with our simultaneous arrivals in Salt Lake City in 1979. The Jazz had moved their franchise from New Orleans to Salt Lake. The next season their head athletic trainer, Don Sparks, called Bill Bean to see if he had an up-and-coming student athletic trainer that would want to be a part-time assistant for the Jazz. Sparky and Bill Bean knew each other because they were both in the ABA together. Sparky was with the Memphis Tams, and the Miami Floridians and Bill was with the Utah Stars.

Bean recommended me, and I jumped at the opportunity. I had already met Don Sparks and the entire Jazz staff when they would come to Victoria Station, where I bartended in the evenings. They knew I was studying sports medicine because I always had a textbook under the bar. When it was slow, I would study. I was able to get to know head coach Tom Nissalke, assistant coach Gene Littles and general manager, Frank Layden.

But the most important life-lasting relationship I made there came from my meeting, Bill Bertka. He had been the GM of the New Orleans Jazz when they made the deal to get Pistol Pete Maravich in 1971, and he came with them to Utah. Bertka's history with the Lakers went all the way back to 1968 when he was a scout. So when Pat Riley became the Lakers head coach in 1980 and needed an assistant, Bertka was the first call he made. The Lakers were looking to hire a new head athletic trainer in 1984, and it was Bertka that went to bat for me. I will forever be in debt to him for the Lakers opportunity, but it's deeper than that. I sat next to Bill on the bench for many years, and most of what I know about the pro game came from Bill. He was also a great friend and mentor, and when there were tough decisions to make, I always ask myself: would Bill approve? Bertka opened the door to Pat Riley, Jerry West and the Los Angeles Lakers for me and I walked through it. The Italian American kid with a failed high school sports career found himself amid sports greatness. The rest is a 32-year history of working side by side with Hall of Famers while going to the NBA finals 12 times and walking away with 8 championship rings.

If you don't like where you're at, have the courage and work ethic to change it!

CHAPTER 4

TO THINE OWN SELF BE TRUE

Says Polonius in Hamlet from the words of William Shakespeare: "To thine own self be true."

Your leader doesn't always have to be the best player on the team, but it sure helps if he is. Your leader should be the extension of the coach, the equivalent of having a coach on the floor and it sure helps if he's a good guy. Being a good guy means being an honest guy. Over the years, I had players that got coaches fired, teammates traded and even slept with their teammate's girlfriends. They may have appeared to the fan base that they were great guys and great teammates.

But they weren't.

Most of their teammates would bend to their will because of the power they held with the coach and the front office. But some players had the intestinal fortitude to stand up to them, believing that it would be better to get traded than to live in an atmosphere based on a lie.

In my later years, because of the increasing age difference, I became more of a mentor than a contemporary. When we would sign a player that was supposed to have leadership qualities I would wait for the appropriate time and then present him with this scenario: I wanted him to picture a window frame with four panes of glass:

1. In pane one I want you to put how you see yourself.
2. In pane two I want you to put how you think other people see you.
3. In pane three I want you to put how other people really see you.
4. In pane four, I want you to put how you really are.

Think of the possible permutations of these four variables. The four panes can be completely different from each other, or they can all be the same. If they are the same, you are very true to yourself. Hence the Greek aphorism: know thyself. For people to follow you, they must know the true you. And to know the true you, you must know your true self. I'm not as eloquent or precise as Shakespeare, but you get the idea.

You can't get around this exercise to determine if you are true to yourself. Kareem was a man that was true to himself. He didn't play his teammates, the media, or the public. There was no big broad smile while he shoved a knife in your back. If you were going to get the knife from him, you were going to get it in the chest. The real good guy on the team doesn't have to be the most vocal. But he must be the one most true to himself.

My first experience working in the NBA was with the Utah Jazz. It was a team without a true leader. When a team does not have a player as a leader, then the head coach has to become one. This is hard on a coach, I've never been involved with a successful team that didn't have a player as a leader.

Arriving at the Lakers organization in 1984, I found that there was leadership and it came from the quietest member of the team, Kareem Abdul-Jabbar. Kareem was not a rah-rah kind of guy. Indeed, most of his teammates walked on eggshells around him. But there was never ever a doubt about who and what Kareem was. He was a true champion with the titles, honors, and awards to back it up.

I could make an argument that Kareem was not only the greatest basketball player to ever play the game, but he may be the most successful athlete to ever walk the planet. The young players in the NBA today never had the opportunity to see him play and many fans that only saw him towards the end of his career don't appreciate just how dominant he was in his prime.

The following is a list of the big fella's accomplishments. I

53

don't think there is an athlete in the history of any sport that compares to this in totality:

6 x NBA Champion

2 x NBA Finals Most Valuable Player

6 x NBA Most Valuable Player

19 x NBA All-Star

10 x All NBA First Team

5 x All NBA Second Team

5 X All NBA Defensive First Team

6 X All NBA Defensive Second Team

NBA Rookie of the Year

2 x NBA Scoring Champion

1 x NBA Rebounding Champion

4 x NBA Blocks Leader
Voted to NBA top 50 of All Time

3 x NCAA Champion

3 x NCAA Final Four Most Outstanding Player

3 x National College Player of the Year
3 x Consensus First Team All American

2 x Mr. Basketball USA
Inducted into the College Basketball Hall of Fame

Inducted into the Naismith Memorial Basketball Hall of Fame

And is currently the all-time NBA leading career scoring Champion. And probably always will be.

Kareem played for 20 seasons in the NBA. During that time his teams made the playoffs 18 times and reached the Finals 10 times. The Showtime era Lakers never won another championship without him.

As dozens of sportswriters have pointed out over the years, Kareem wasn't always the most welcoming and pleasant guy in the room. But he was still the epitome of grace to not only me but my family as well.

He probably wouldn't remember this one particular incident, but I certainly do. We were staying at the Boston Marriott Copley Square for the 1985 Finals. The lobby was packed with both Lakers and Celtics fans. Security was lax, and there was no one to stop anyone from getting on an elevator going up to the player's floor. An elevator would open, and there was a rush of people trying to get on with the players. My mom and dad, who were in their 60's at the time, were getting shoved around in the crowd. They were saved by Kareem. He held the elevator door and pushed people out of the way and said Mr. and Mrs. Vitti, please get on with me. Kareem made it easy for the press to put a target on his back. But if you're looking for the truth, it's Kareem Abdul-Jabbar who will deliver it.

****

After Kareem left, it took us 12 years before we were able to hoist another banner. We had talent that came and went, and we even had superstars -- but they had yet to become true leaders.

In 1999 without a player as a true leader, our new head coach Phil Jackson became the leader, not by choice but by necessity. As time passed, he tried to pass the baton to Kobe and Shaq. The problem was they both wanted that baton for themselves. And they were drastically different types of leaders. I believe they were true to themselves in terms of the 4 window panes, but because of their contrasting natures, it was hard for team members to choose one to follow. Shaq was this great, fun-loving big kid but he didn't want to put in the daily grind that his teammates were expected to do. The problem was that he was so dominating when he wanted to play hard that he and his teammates knew we couldn't win without him. On the other hand, there's Kobe. Someone who had the work ethic and the competitive spirit that earned the respect of his teammates. I have been with winning teams that on an off night, all went to the movies together. The chemistry was great on and off the court - and they won.

I have also been with teams that had a 15-man roster, and after the game, 15 different cabs were going in 15 different directions. But on the court, they played together, as a team - and they also won.

That was more like the Lakers teams of 2000, 2001 and 2002. It worked, but eventually, it caught up to us. We had a team that could have won championships for a decade but instead we self-imploded in just 4 years.

There's plenty of blame to go around. Although it's easy to point fingers at Shaq and Kobe, it's also unfair. They didn't own the personality tools to get out of their own way – or of each other. There should have been an intervention by the coach or even by upper management. But instead they were pitted against each other, and people picked sides. When people choose sides on a team, it's divisive, and the alpha comes out, and we had two alphas.

In 2003 Shaq had just been the MVP of the last three NBA Finals in a row. He was feeling like he was the man so much so that he made a decision that might have made sense to him -- but not to anyone else. Not to management, not to his teammates and -- most crucially for his image -- not to the fans.

Shaq had a legitimate issue with his big toe that required surgery. In his defense, trying to push off your big toe with the problem he had can be extremely painful – especially when you're carrying 350 pounds.

But he had plenty of time to have the corrective surgery following the finals and still be ready for training camp. A regular NBA season ends around the second week of April. What follows is the longest 10 weeks of your life trying to win a championship. Followed by the shortest 15 weeks of your life before training camp, and the grind starts all over again.

I'm not justifying what Shaq did. But I understand. It's hard enough to win an NBA title even once. But to do it 3 times in a row as we had just done can distort your thinking.

So, Shaq did the unthinkable. He told the press he got hurt on company time so he'll rehab on company time. Knowing him the way I do, I'm sure he would never make the same decision with what he knows about life today. But at the time it was sacrilege, and neither the basketball Gods or basketball fans honor sacrilege.

The whole thing might have been swept under the carpet as things are in sports when you win, but that year we didn't win. Without Shaq, we got off to a slow 3 - 9 start and didn't improve much when he returned. We were 11 - 19 thirty games into the season -- the Lakers' worst start in a decade. We finished 5th in the west and lost to the Spurs in the second round of the playoffs. To make matters worse for Shaq in the court of both public and private opinion his co-captain Kobe Bryant played all 82 games.The Lakers needed to make a move, and we did. We signed Gary Payton and Karl Malone. We now had 4 future Hall of Famers ready to make another run at the title. But Dr. Buss and Shaq were in the middle of contract negotiations, and it wasn't going well. Shaq felt like he was the man and yet was not being respected. The rest of the world felt that Shaq didn't care about winning and only cared about money.

Then Shaq made his second big blunder as a Laker. The Lakers were at the University of Hawaii for training camp. We practiced and played two pre-season games at the Stan Sheriff Center, named after UH's former athletic director.

After one of Shaq's signature monster dunks that sent the capacity crowd into an uproar, he ran by and stared down our owner and yelled: "pay me, pay me." Dr. Buss didn't flinch. He didn't get to where he was in life by being intimidated by anyone. He once told me during one of our heart-to-heart talks that he was in a contract negotiation with Kareem at his home called Pickfair. Pickfair was the famed Beverly Hills estate built by Douglas Fairbanks for the famous silent movie actress, Mary Pickford. He told me that during their negotiation, Kareem said "You need me" and his response, as he looked around his Pickfair estate, was: "Look around, Kareem. I don't need anyone. That's what this is all about."

Things hadn't changed. Dr. Buss was not one to be intimidated -- all four of his window panes of truth were all the same. But Shaq was also true to himself. His four panes were all the same as well. And so he asked to be traded. After our 4-1 Finals loss to the Detroit Pistons, Dr. Buss was happy to accommodate him. We sent him to Miami for Caron Butler, Brian Grant, and Lamar Odom. He ultimately led the Miami Heat to his 4th NBA championship in 2006.

Shaq did many things wrong that I know he would change if he could. But people followed Shaq because, beyond his sheer physical dominance, there was nothing fake about

58

him. You knew where you stood with him: good, bad, or indifferent. Shaq's failures with the Lakers were also the Laker's failures. Neither he nor Kobe received the structural support to fix what was broken. In the words of the famous writer, political activist and early black panther leader, Eldridge Clever: "*If you're not part of the solution, you are part of the problem.*"

We blame Shaq and Kobe for the implosion of that team, but the Lakers' entire organization was just as much a part of the problem because we were not part of the solution.Despite what you think of them, Kobe and Shaq were true to themselves. There was nothing fake about them, and although neither one made it easy, it was not wholly their fault, and I cherish my relationship with both of them. I don't think I could have been the one to have saved the situation, but I can't help but think I could have done better? I wasn't part of the solution, which means I was part of the problem. When you have a team that can win it all, you must do everything you can do to win it. A lost opportunity is precisely what it was -- lost. Once lost, it's gone forever. If you don't want to go through life thinking, "What if" - you better seize the moment of opportunity and capitalize on it.

To thine own self be true.

CHAPTER 5

THE SECRET TO HAPPINESS

The worst period of my life begins with the most mysterious phone call of my life.

It's October 24, 1991. My favorite time of year: training camp. We've all had a summer to rest and recuperate after yet another trip to the NBA Finals – the fifth time in my seven seasons as the LA Lakers head athletic trainer. Now everyone is revving up for a new season and another run to the Finals.

We've even got a new mission: *Beat the Bulls*.

After losing to Michael Jordan and the Chicago Bulls in the 1991 NBA Finals, it's clear that the Bulls have replaced the Boston Celtics and Detroit Pistons as the team we will have to beat in the 1990s to enjoy the same kind of dominance that we had in the '80s.

We even have a new coach, former NBA player Mike Dunleavy, to fill the void left by Pat Riley when he departed after the 1990 season. Riley resigned either voluntarily or involuntarily, depending on who you talk to. It was very messy both privately and publicly, so I'm not sure exactly how it all went down. Either way, it was clear that after producing four championships in eight years Riley's micro-managing, and ultra-demanding style had finally lost its effectiveness. The players needed to hear a new voice. But personally, I was sad to see him go. He hired me on a hunch, taught me his secrets of leadership, and inspired me to keep expanding my skill-set. In my view, he was an intense guy, but he was always respectful and never tried to embarrass anyone. The rest of the team structure that helped the Lakers dominate the '80's remains intact. Owner Dr. Jerry Buss is a smart, hands-off guy who hires great employees and empowers them. On the few occasions he shows up at practices, he commands respect among the players and staff just by his very presence. Then there's General Manager Jerry West, the Hall of Fame player who turned himself into the best sports executive in the business.

He can see around corners, anticipate problems, and find solutions before the rest of us even realize there's a problem. And of course we still have the Showtime trio of Magic Johnson, James Worthy, and Byron Scott – two can't-miss Hall of Famers and an elite shooting guard.

As long as we have them, we will always be a championship contender. Granted, Kareem Abdul Jabbar has retired as the leading scorer in NBA history. But Magic has taken young Yugoslav center Vlade Divac on as a personal project, and he is showing great promise. Also, talented power forward Elden Campbell is taking up much of Kareem's rebounding responsibilities, and Sam Perkins gives us a three-point shooting big man that is also a low post defender.

After a grueling trip to Paris where we win the McDonald's Cup with a last-second victory over Spain, we're back in the States. We only have two more exhibition games, one in Utah and one in Vancouver, before the regular-season opener at the Fabulous Forum in Los Angeles.

Magic calls me at my home. Says he's exhausted and wants to rest up before for the season opener. Can I get him out of these last two pre-season games? I tell him it's fine with me, but I'll have to check with West. West says the Utah game is sold out, but the Vancouver game is not. The league wants to expand and put a team in Vancouver. They've been advertising Magic as the star attraction for the game. So, for the sake of our relationship with the league and Commissioner David Stern, Magic needs to play, at least in Vancouver. I relay the terrible news to Magic. He's not happy but says if he has to play one game, he might as well play both. I feel bad that I couldn't deliver for him. I did my best to get him some rest because he deserves it. Not only is he the leader and the best player on the team but he's also the hardest worker. That doesn't happen very often on any side – high school, college, or the NBA. The next morning, we fly to Salt Lake City. At the hotel I find a bunch of messages to call West ASAP. Up until now, every discussion I've ever had with West was direct and informative. He never withheld anything from me, as far as I know, which is one among many reasons that I hold him in such high regard. But this call is different. West is direct – "Get Magic on a plane back to LA as soon as possible," -- but definitely not informative. I ask him why Magic needs to return, and he uncharacteristically brushes me off. Something's up, but I have no idea what in the world it could be. I call Magic. Turns out he already got the same "come-home" message from the Lakers team doctor, Michael Mellman. I ask him what's going on.

Magic: "I don't know. I thought you could tell me."
GV: "I got nothing for you, man."

So I arrange for a first-class ticket back to LA, put him in a cab, and send him back home. But as I get the players ready for the game against the Jazz, my mind won't stop circling around one burning question: why is Magic suddenly needed back in LA 24 hours after they insisted that he had to play in these last pre-season games. Is it some medical problem? Cancer? Some previously undetected heart problem? We already got all his blood panels back, and anything negative would have been known before now. So why the sudden change in plans?

We're beating the Jazz, but I'm not really paying attention. My mind is focused on figuring out the reason for Magic's sudden departure. Then early in the second quarter, it all comes together in an epiphany that screams out the answer. Besides our standard NBA physical exam, Magic had just had a second physical exam for a life insurance policy. The only difference between the NBA exam and the insurance exam: we are not allowed to test for the Human Immunodeficiency Virus, but for life insurance, it's required. It's just one of those times when the light bulb goes off, and the answer is glaringly apparent

63

even though at the same time it's shocking and unbelievable: Magic must have tested positive for the HI virus on the insurance exam. There are few secrets in a pro sports locker room, so I know he's been with many, many women over the last 10 years and hasn't always practiced safe sex. He loves the ladies, and the ladies love him. As he often told me, he always did his best to "accommodate" them.

Damn it, I should have insisted he always use a condom, but somehow the topic never came up. I let him down. Preaching safe sex is not a traditional part of the athletic trainer's job, but I like to think I'm not a conventional athletic trainer. Not just a guy who tapes ankles. I prided myself on the idea that Riley hired me because I was an innovative guy on the cutting edge of sports medicine, fitness, and nutrition. But this time I wasn't innovative enough.

Instantly it's all I can think about: Magic Johnson – our teammate, captain, and superstar -- is now facing a death sentence. After all, in the few years since HIV and AIDS emerged as a public health issue, that's been the accepted narrative: if you get the HI virus, you're inevitably going to get AIDS and then you're going to die quickly and ugly. You'll suffer a wasting away process that destroys healthy young people in a matter of weeks or months.

A deep, dense fog settles over my brain. I've always been a pretty intuitive guy, and I've learned to trust my instincts. In my gut, I know Magic must have tested HIV positive. I can't explain how or why I am so sure, but I am. I still have to do my job, but now I'm operating on auto-pilot. I'm still there physically, but mentally, there's no one home.

During the game, one of our rookie guards, Tony Smith from Marquette, blows his ankle out. We carry him into the locker room and put him on the training table for treatment. It's a third-degree sprain. It's blowing up with swelling right before our eyes, and it's clear he's going to be out for a while. He is very upset, which is not the first time I have seen a player lose it over an injury. He's worked so hard to get his shot at the NBA, and now this shit happens.

Still thinking about Magic, I tell Smith that he's going to recover from his injury, but some sick people in the world are never going to get better. Of course, I am thinking about Magic, but he doesn't know that. I can't elaborate and tell him about Magic. I can't tell anyone about Magic. At this point, it's just a hunch. A very, very strong hunch. After the game, we fly to Vancouver. Once I'm settled into the Pan Pacific Hotel, I can't sleep at all. I toss and turn all night. I'm up and out of bed at the crack of dawn. I pull the curtains back and look out the picture window. The hotel is a magnificent place over-looking the ocean. Seaplanes are landing, squawking seagulls are strutting on the beach. I'm struck by the contrast between the stunning beauty of the place and the complete sense of dread overwhelming me. The phone rings.

It's Dr. Mellman, a guy I work with closely. We're used to talking about sensitive health issues. I can't hold back.

GV: "Magic's HIV positive, isn't he?"
Mellman: "I knew you would figure it out…Look, Magic wanted you to know about it, that's why I'm calling. But he also asks that you not tell anybody. And we need you to come in and get screened as soon as you get back to LA."

GV: "What are we going to say about all this?"
Mellman: "We're going to say he's got the flu."

Now we have to tell a lie to the rest of the team, our families, our friends - and the rest of the world.

After 24 hours in the dark, I'm back in the loop. The problem is, I don't want to be in this loop. Dr. Mellman told me there

65

are only seven people who know this terrible secret: me, Mell-man, Magic, his wife Cookie – they've been married all of six weeks – West, Dr. Buss, and Magic's agent, Lon Rosen.

After the game in Vancouver, we fly home to LA. Early the next morning, I meet Magic at Loyola Marymount University, where we often practice. We hug without saying a word. He knows I know. I take out my keys and open the locker room. It's just him and me in there, so I ask him how he's handling his shocking diagnosis. Is he OK? I ask because I'm not OK. I tell him I can't sleep, can't eat, and basically can't function. He grabs me by the shoulders and looks me straight in the eye without a hint of self-pity and says: "When God gave me this disease, he gave it to the right person. I'm going to do some-thing really good with this."

It is a moment imprinted on my heart and soul forever. At a time when I am devastated, Magic is showing me how he handles the worst kind of adversity: keep your head up, keep marching forward, and always look for the positive. This gen-uinely stunning declaration triggers contradictory emotions in me. I am so proud of Magic for taking such a courageous, pro-active approach. That's the man I've known and respect-ed as a true champion for the last seven years. But I also think to myself, don't you get it, man? You are going to die, and it's going to be an ugly death. He sounds like he is in total denial, which just sends me deeper into depression.

After we part with another silent hug, the team shows up for practice, and I perform my usual duties like a zombie athletic trainer. I feel like I'm having an out-of-body experience. This really can't be happening. It feels surreal.

I get my HIV screening, and it comes back negative. Not sur-prising but good to know. After my screening, I faintly start to sense an emotion that silently grows and grows over the next few weeks and months until it becomes a big part of my personal philosophy: your good health and that of your loved ones is the most essential thing in life. Good health is taken for granted, but when you lose it, everything else in the world becomes inconsequential by comparison.

I start to realize on a subliminal level that the secret to happiness is being grateful for what you have and that it begins with being thankful for your good health. The problem is that I'm experiencing so many negative emotions over Magic's diagnosis that on the surface, I mainly feel depressed and disoriented: how could this be happening to such a healthy, vibrant guy? But down deep in my soul, this life-affirming belief that good health is the ultimate gift is slowly taking hold, although it doesn't emerge fully formed for a few months. That's because my brain fog isn't lifting at all as the team spends the next two weeks preparing for the regular-season opener. Magic is out of sight but not out of mind. At least once a day, a player or media member asks me where he is and when he's coming back. By rote, I repeat the out-with-the-flu cover story, and everybody seems to accept it – because I've never lied to them before. In the past, when I couldn't tell the press something, I would simply say I can't comment on that subject, and they respected my honesty.

Now my hard-won credibility is being used to sell a lie.

Finally the regular season starts and Magic misses the first three games. I can't even spill the secret to Chick Hearn, the Lakers legendary broadcaster, my mentor and a good friend. It's painful to hear him telling his listeners about Magic being out with flu-like symptoms. My deception has now become his deception. We are lying to the world. And I can't help but wonder how long until our dark secret leaks out. Like I said, very few secrets survive for long in a pro sports locker room. The players are in such close proximity to each other, and writers and TV guys are coming around their lockers every day to ask questions. And this is no normal secret. I'm media-savvy enough to understand that this is a news nuclear bomb of epic proportions, an international story that will explode on the media landscape if and when it gets out: Magic, the most beloved athlete in America, the very picture of heterosexual virility, is infected with HIV, up till now known primarily as "the gay disease". I fear the media and the public will ignore the medical nuances and rush to a conclusion: Magic has AIDS! Can you freakin' believe it? Every shock jock and sports show yacker in the country will dwell on all the lurid angles: how did he get it? Is he secretly gay? How long till he dies? Who has he passed it on to? I just know it's going to be the biggest nightmare the Lakers have ever lived through.

Dr. Mellman tells me the Lakers have already had Magic re-tested for the HI virus and are now anxiously awaiting the results. But he says the chances of a false positive on the initial insurance exam are very low. We should assume this second test will just confirm the first. Then what's the next step? Should we tell everyone or tell no one? Should Magic keep playing as if nothing has changed – after all, he still looks and acts the same as always – or should he retire to deal with the virus coursing through his body?

A couple days later I have phone conversations with Dr. Mellman and Magic's agent, Lon Rosen. The seven people that know about Magic are all shattered by this news – I'm told West has been seen crying about it – but from my perspective, we can't stay paralyzed once we get the expected confirmation. I've thought about it every day and every night and feel very strongly that we have no choice: we have to go public, and we have to do it as soon as possible. We simply don't know who Magic has had sex with. We don't know who they are, what their names are, or how to get in touch with them to alert them that they need to get tested for HIV.

For all we know, he has spread the virus to them, and now they are unknowingly spreading it to others while we keep the secret to ourselves. Every day that passes in silence just raises the stakes more. That leaves us only one choice, as painful as it is: a public announcement.

Two weeks go by after my emotional meeting with Magic at Loyola Marymount. The tension inside me is building to a breaking point. How long can I go on like this? Finally, I get a call from Rosen on Tuesday, November 5. He says the Lakers have carefully constructed a plan for Magic to break the news to the public Friday while the rest of the team is flying to our first road game of the season. He says Magic wants me to get the team into a conference room at LAX where he will tell the team about his diagnosis. Then he will leave the airport and go to the Great Western Forum where he will hold a press conference.

I don't tell anybody anything about this plan, but it makes me feel a little better. At least we are going to deal with it in a responsible manner that will soften the blow to Magic's team-mates, alert the women that need to know and try to mini-mize the public uproar. Thursday morning we're practicing at Loyola Marymount when I get a call from West. He says there's been a leak. It's being announced on the radio that Magic has tested positive for HIV. He tells me to get the play-ers out of the gym right away. I'm to tell them not to talk to the media, and to gather at the Forum at 2:00 this afternoon. No exceptions: everyone must be there!

I go back out and gather the coaches and the players for a short message: I can't tell you what's going on, but I need you to all get in your cars and leave as soon as possible. Don't talk to any media, and go to the Forum for a 2:00 pm press conference. There's some grumbling from a couple of players that they have stuff they planned to do this afternoon, so I de-cide on my own to go a little further than West had instructed. "Look, I can't tell you everything, but I can tell you that what you hear today will change your life forever...Your life will never be the same." That gets their attention and everyone heads out to the parking lot.

I drive straight to the Forum, where the players are already gathering. There's a buzz in the room, and I realize that some guys had their radios on in the car, on their way to the Forum while other guys were listening to music. So now some guys knew what was being reported and some guys didn't. It feels strange to be in a room where half the guys know about Magic, and half the guys don't know, so I gather the whole team and tell them that there are radio reports that Magic has HIV and he's going to come talk to you about it.

Minutes later, Magic walks in, and the whole room goes silent. No one knows what to say. How could they? None of us has ever faced a situation like this before. The room is grim, far grimmer than I've ever seen before, no matter how bad the situation the Lakers were facing. Magic breaks the silence by talking about all the battles we've been through together. Facing down the Celtics in '85 when they had the hex on us for so many years. Beating the Pistons in '88 for a repeat title. And he emphasizes how much his teammates mean to him as brothers. Then he lowers the volume to confirm the news that was being reported on the radio: he's tested positive for HIV. Then he adds the kicker: he's going to retire to focus on dealing with the disease.

The silence in the room gets even louder. You can see each player digesting what this means. Like me two weeks ago, most of them perceive it as a death sentence for their leader. You can just tell by the looks on their faces. At this point, they're not even thinking about his sudden retirement and what it means for them and for the team.

Pro sports tends to foster a me-first mentality – and who can blame them when players only get paid for production and are quickly discarded as soon as they are no longer useful – but

70

that all disappears in this room. The hurt, the fear, and the despair hang in the air like freeway smog. Sensing this, Magic – of all people – transcends the moment to lift the mood. One by one, he approaches each person in the room, gives them a big hug and whispers something only they can hear. One of the truly amazing things I noticed about Magic right from the start of my association with him was his uncanny ability always to say the right thing to make people feel better. This gift carries him through an emotional gauntlet. Second to last is assistant coach Bill Bertka, the man who recommended me to Riley when he was looking for a new athletic trainer back in '84. Bill and I are best friends, and I know that he is a stoic man who has been through a lot in life, has seen a lot in life, and as a result, rarely shows any emotion. I'm standing next to him now, awaiting my hug when I notice that Bill's knees are buckling and he starts crying as he slumps to the ground. Magic reaches out with his huge arms and pulls him back up and whispers to him as he steadies him. As Magic approaches me, I'm still stunned by Bertka's totally uncharacteristic collapse. I speak first: "It's OK, brother. You and I have already done this." As he gathers me up for a big hug – at 6-foot-9, he's a full foot taller than me – he whispers back: "Yeah, but that doesn't make it any easier."

After I've recovered – after we've all recovered – Magic heads upstairs to the press conference and we all follow him. Then we stand in the back of the room and watch him perform one of the most courageous public acts I have ever seen. Totally poised, with the usual Magic charm, he tells the world that he has tested positive for HIV and will have to retire. The sheer shock of the news ricochets around the world in record time. Magic walks away with Cookie at his side and the Showtime era – launched in the 1979-80 season when the rookie Magic led the Lakers to a world title – is suddenly over.

I begin to rethink the buying into the American sports creed that there is winning and there is misery, and there's nothing in between. I start to think that it's good to chase things and it's good to want more, but your happiness should not rely on it. In our case, we were chasing championships to make us happy. I realized that I lived this yoyo life of the thrill of victory and the agony of defeat until that eventful day that we learned Magic Johnson converted sero-positive for HIV.

I see it clearly that being in the health care field for more than half of my life, I saw people lose their health, and when they did everything terrible in their lives became inconsequential. I discover that the secret to happiness is to be grateful for what you have, and that begins with your health and that of your loved ones. If you have that, you have never been better in your life.

For many of us, our adult lives began when we went to college, and we thought about how hard life is, studying, taking tests, no money. We say to ourselves I just need to graduate, and then I will be happy. You finally get through it, but now you need a job, a reward for all of your hard work in school. You just need a foot in the door, and then I'll be happy. You find that job, and you're happy for a short period. Now you're making a few dollars, but you need a new car. You've been driving that beater around since college. You get a new car and then you are happy for a short period.

Then you just need to find someone special to share your life with and you do, and you're happy. But then it's time for a promotion. You get the promotion.
Now you need a house. It doesn't have to be a big house, just a little something you can call your own. You get the house, and then you start having children, so you need a bigger house.

I'll say it again it's good to chase things. It's good to want more. But your happiness should not rely on it. The point is there will always be something else to chase when all this time you already had the real secret of happiness, and it's not achieving what you are chasing. It's being grateful for all the things you already have beginning with your health and that of your loved ones. This is not a talk about health.

It's a talk about your attitude and how you can change the world you live in and work in. Happiness in the workplace is a serious problem, and each of you can change the energy of a workplace with a simple mind shift and a simple answer to the small talk. The small talk is when someone asks, "how you are?". Do they really care how you are, or is it small talk? Is it really a question, or is it just a greeting. If you have your health, and someone asks how you are, the simple mind shift and the simple answer is "never better in my life."

This one simple answer to the small talk will cause a mind shift that can change the entire spirit of a workplace. The question is, can you make people around you better with your attitude and your energy.

You can be healthy and choose to be unhappy, but it's hard to be happy if you are unhealthy. Choose happiness before you have to learn it the hard way as I did. In the face of what we thought was a death sentence, Magic chose to make people around him better. Shouldn't we do the same?

CHAPTER 6

LAUGH A LITTLE EACH DAY

It may look like it's all fun and games and glamour to the fans. But for players, coaches and executives alike there is one common denominator: pro basketball is a serious business. The season runs from the beginning of training camp in September to the last regular-season game in mid-April. Then the playoffs begin. But even if you don't make the playoffs, it doesn't stop. There are the Combines to evaluate players and then the player draft itself in late June. Most teams are bringing in 70, 80 or even 100 players for pre-draft workouts, so if your team is in the playoffs, you're doing double duty. After the draft, there is summer league followed by a short, less stressful time during August. But even then the training room, weight room, and gym are open and manned every day. By Labor Day teams are operating full tilt getting ready for training camp again. All this time, jobs are on the line, careers are made, and legacies are defined. It's a 12-months-a-year grind for glory -- and for a paycheck far more significant than that earned by 99% of the general population.

But one of the things I firmly believed as the Lakers head athletic trainer is that you gotta have some fun, gotta have some belly laughs while you're going about the serious business of trying to make the team or trying to help the team win a championship. Like any workplace in any profession, lightening the mood occasionally is good for staff morale and great for office productivity.

There always seemed to be some guys on the team that are the biggest jokesters. In the 80's it was James Worthy, Byron Scott, and Orlando Woolridge. You needed to have thick skin around these guys. God forbid you had something wrong with you like big ears or a big nose. They looked for your vulnerability and went right at you.

We used to have this moronic game called the paper game. It wouldn't be uncommon for us to be in a commercial airline terminal sprawled out in a seat with your face buried reading the sports page when a player would walk up to you and ka-rate chop the paper out of your hands. It would startle you, and depending on how tightly you were holding the paper, it could tear in half. It was a stupid and childish game, but it took on a life where guys were folding the paper to make it small enough not to be a target. At one time or another, every-one got their paper swatted. The only exception was Kareem Abdul-Jabbar. Kareem was above such childishness and no-body messed with him.

One day we were in the locker room at the Forum, and Ka-reem was reading his paper wide open at his locker. Michael Cooper's locker was next to Magic Johnson, and Coop leans over and says I'll give you $100.00 if you smack that paper out of Kareem's hands. Magic said $100.00...shiiit. He got up and walked over and swatted that paper right out of Kareem's hands. Everyone wanted to laugh but were afraid. Kareem, showing zero emotion, calmly looked up and said: "I heard that, Coop." His unspoken message was that the payback was coming to Coop for instigating it. Not to Magic for actually doing the deed.

Months passed without retaliation, but just because nothing happened yet, it didn't mean it wasn't going to. Kareem was calculating and had a memory of anyone that dissed him. Fi-nally, one day we were on a Northwest Airlines flight out of Detroit when Kareem decided it was time. Coop was always a hard sleeper on the plane and slept with a blanket over his head. Kareem quietly got up, pulled the blanket off his head, and gently put a large dab of Nair on top of Coop's head just above his hairline. Within minutes Coop's head was on fire, and there was a nickel-sized area of hair burned off.

That was the end of the paper game.

It was replaced by the luggage game. During the days of com-mercial flights, our luggage came out with everyone else's on the plane. Per diem was $25.00 a day. So each player would put up $5.00 to see who's bag would come out of baggage claim first. Other passengers would want to get in on the game when they would see the players gathered around a big pile of money on the floor in front of the carousel. No one could get hurt from this game, and someone was walking away with some extra pocket money, usually Bill Bertka.

The thing that I miss the most now after retiring in 2016 is the camaraderie and the ridiculous things people say and do. There's nothing better than when a team has chemistry, and they share the crazy moments and the spontaneous, laugh-out-loud locker room times.

Shaq was one of those guys who could make you laugh even when he didn't mean to. You never knew what was going to come out of his mouth. He went to Athens, Greece, one summer and someone asked him if he had been to the Parthenon, the former temple on the Athenian Acropolis built in 447 BC and still standing as a cultural landmark. "I don't know," he replied. "I can't remember all the clubs we went to."

Or the time that James Worthy was raving to a reporter about the non-verbal communication he had with Magic Johnson on the court, recalling how Magic knew where to pass the ball even before James made his move to the hoop. "Yeah," Magic chimed in. "It's like we've got ESPN."

A live game is not exempt from such moments. There was a twenty-second time out in the middle of one game because Sedale Threatt got hurt. It's always good if you can see the injury happen, but sometimes you miss it and have to ask the player what happened. I ran out there in front of 20 thousand people in the stands and millions more watching the game on TV. I asked Sedale where he got hurt and instead of telling me where on his body he was injured, he pointed to the spot on the floor and said: "I got hurt over there." Trying not to laugh, I said: "No, on your body, where did you get hurt?" He answered, "GV, my shit be broke!" Still trying not to laugh but needing to figure out what's wrong with the guy I replied: "Is it your left shit or your right shit?" He replied, left. It felt like I was practicing veterinary medicine. You know there is something wrong with your cat or dog but they can't tell you what it is.

The all-time quote I was not ready for was on the bench during a game. Pat Riley was coaching from the sideline when he was distracted by something between the players on the bench. He turned around and told me to go find out what was going on down there. As I walked down the sidelines, the players started pointing to one of their teammates. I asked him what's going on? He shucked his shoulders and said, I'm fine. I responded by telling him that the coach knows something is going on and he sent me down here to find out so what should I tell him. The player looked me directly in the eye, and with a straight face, his exact words were "I shit myself." I was at a loss for words, so I said well go in the back and get yourself cleaned up. To which he replied, Nah I'm ok! There was nothing in my education and experience as an athletic trainer that prepared me for that!

Factor in that you are dealing with young, fun-loving males, often with a lot of money for the first time in their lives, and you have a recipe for some crazy things to happen. And living and working in the glitz and glamour of Los Angeles just make the possibilities for mischief even more volatile.

I am not going to reveal the name of a player who got royally pranked other than to say that he was a reserve who rarely played and in fact didn't even dress for most of the games. He usually had to sit in the row of seats behind the player's bench, sporting a suit and tie. But we have to call him something, so let's call him Player X.

I swear to you that this story is 100 percent true. Only one name has been changed to protect the not-so-innocent fool who brought all this craziness down on himself. He bragged about something that wasn't actually happening and then doubled down on it. When his teammates challenged him, he missed his chance to come clean and suffered the consequences.

It all started with the return to LA of Vlade Divac, who was drafted by the Lakers in 1989 and traded to Charlotte in 1996 for the draft rights to Kobe Bryant – the greatest trade in Lakers history. A decade later he came back to LA after helping lead the Sacramento Kings teams to challenge the Lakers during the three-peat years from 2000-02. Now he was finishing up his career with the Lakers in a sentimental homecoming, but he suffered a prolapsed disc that required surgery. So for much of the season, he sat on the bench, out of uniform. As a long-term veteran, he was given priority for the bench seats over younger players like Player X, who had to sit behind the bench with a couple of other guys who weren't playing.

One night at Staples Center Player X somehow got it in his head that the talented and beautiful actress Lucy Liu, who rose to fame in the TV series Ally McBeal and had been appearing in films and TV shows ever since, was giving him the sweet eye from her courtside seat on the baseline next to our bench.

So Player X started bugging Vlade all during the first half to switch seats with him so he could be closer to the actress. "Dude, Lucy Liu is checking me out! You gotta give me your seat," he said several times. At first, Vlade just told him to get lost. Finally, he got so sick of listening to his whining that as the second half started he said: "Ok, sit here if you want it so bad." After they switched seats, Vlade saw an opening for a great practical joke, the kind most players love to pull off. He gave the female usher his phone and asked her to record a new voice mail message. "But instead of it being me, say that you're Lucy Liu." No problem. So now Vlade's phone had a female's voice with a new message: "You've reached Lucy Liu. I can't come to the phone right now. Please leave a message." Then Vlade wrote out his number, gave it to the usher and asked her to give it to Player X and say it's from Lucy Liu.

Naturally, Player X came in the locker room showing everyone the note and quickly started calling her, but she never picked up the phone. Instead when he would leave a voice mail Vlade would text him back as if he was Lucy Liu. Player X would then show the text to everyone on the team to prove that he and Lucy Liu were an item. They developed an intense texting relationship, without actually talking to each other. Player X continued telling everyone on the team that he was dating Lucy Liu, that she sent a car for him and that they went out to dinner. Of course, it was all bullshit.

Meanwhile, they kept texting, so Vlade got to see all of Player X's texts. The funniest one was when he asked: "So, Lucy Liu… what is your last name anyway?" We're laughing our asses off at how clueless this kid is, and what a bull-shitter he is. This goes on for two weeks, and by now the whole squad is in on the joke. What had started as a practical joke that would last a day or two had morphed into something far bigger that looked like it could go on for months – all because the kid was living in an alternate universe and trying to convince us it was really real. Lamar Odom, who has the sweetest, softest heart of any athlete I've ever been around, couldn't take it anymore as he watched everyone laughing at Player X behind his back.

Lamar felt terrible for the kid and wanted to tell him ; "Listen, man, you're making an ass out of yourself". But the next day in the trainer's room Kobe started working the kid. He asked Player X, "When you two go out, who pays?" Player X replied: "Shiiit, I'm a pimp, I don't pay. She pays." And that's when Lamar said "This motherfucker! You know what? I'm not gonna let him off the hook." So the "joke" went on. And on. Each day Player X had new updates on all the crazy things he was doing with and to Lucy Liu. Vlade even got the team's Public Relations Department in on it. The PR people got a People Magazine cover and photoshopped it to put Lucy Liu's picture in the corner with a caption that she was dating NBA's, Player X. So what does Player X do? Instead of realizing it was time to end the lies, he got pissed and marched upstairs to the PR department and berated the folks working there, acting like he was a big celebrity whose privacy had been invaded by People Magazine. "You're supposed to protect me from stuff like this," he said. That scene was soon being retold all over Lakers' headquarters.

Finally, Vlade came up with a plan to end it once and for all. He hired a limo and had a camera installed in the back where Player X would be sitting. He texted Player X as "Lucy," saying that she had arranged for a limo to pick him up and that she would be waiting for him at a restaurant in the Pacific Palisades. I still have the video from the camera, so I know exactly what went down. Player X started bragging to the limo driver that he was going to meet Lucy Liu at this fancy restaurant and that she had sent this limo for him. And that afterward they would be going to her place for dessert.

When they pulled up in front of the restaurant, there was a crowd of people milling around outside, as they're often is at these trendy places. But Player X was still living in his fantasy world and asked the driver, "Is that the paparazzi waiting for me and Lucy Liu?"

After making his way through the crowd outside, Player X went into the restaurant to find the whole team waiting for him with a bottle of Dom Perignon on his table, but no Lucy Liu. Guys were cracking up, but he still didn't get it!

Kobe sat in the would-be seat for Lucy Liu, opened up the champagne and started drinking it straight out of the bottle.

81

Then he started grilling Player X on what he was doing there and who he was supposed to meet. Finally, he just blurted it out: "Don't you get it? For weeks we've known this is all bullshit. It's time to cut the crap." But incredibly, Player X doubled down. "No, no, I've been going out with her, I swear I'm dating Lucy Liu."

Well, of course, Lucy Liu never showed up that night, and he finally had to fess up, saying, "Ok, you guys got me." I knew about the set up from the first night Vlade put it in motion, and several times I thought about telling the kid he was being pranked. But as the days went on and I heard him bragging about Lucy Liu, I got so disgusted that I decided to back off and let it play out. It may sound cruel to someone who wasn't there, but he got what he deserved, and the rest of us got a lot of laughs.

There was another funny episode with Player X. It was January 2004, and Google announced they were hiring Morgan Stanley and Goldman Sachs to arrange an IPO. Shaq was ecstatic because he had invested in Google and was about to cash in big-time. While we were all in the training room, Shaq's elation prompted Rick Fox to tell us about his investment woes. The Boston Celtics drafted Foxy in 1991, which put him right at the head of the Dot.com bubble. As a young player with money, he was approached to invest $25,000.00 in Yahoo, which he declined to do. Yahoo went public in 1996 and soon closed up 270% from the IPO price, leaving Foxy with great regret that he never bought into Yahoo. While we all were sharing his pain over this missed opportunity, Player X interjected: "I can see why that stock went up. I used to drink the shit out of that stuff." There was a moment of silence before everyone realized what he said, and the room burst into laughter. Finally, someone said it's Yahoo idiot, not Yoohoo.

Player X wasn't the only player who said funny stuff that wasn't meant to be funny. We were in Dallas one day to play the Mavs at Reunion arena. In those days, we stayed at the Grand Hyatt, which was across the street from the arena. The way the roads ran, we had to take a circuitous route to and from the hotel. That route required us to go through Dealey Plaza, where President Kennedy was assassinated in 1963. As we drove by what is today known as the 6th Floor Museum, one of our players blurted out: "Is that the book suppository?" The entire team bus burst out into laughter. Someone then said it's depository idiot, not suppository.

In 2011 I hired Tim DiFrancesco as the head strength and conditioning coach of the Lakers. Tim was born and raised in Vermont, which is Boston Celtics territory. Growing up, a Celtics fan raised a lot of eyebrows and came up a lot around the weight room. One player heard Tim say he was from New England. He asked Tim: "I thought you were from Vermont?" Tim answered, "Yes, Vermont is in New England." After a moment of confusion and deep thought, the player said: "No, Vermont is in Maine." He was geographically challenged, to say the least.

It's always been interesting to me how some players study the history of the game, and others are completely clueless. On occasion, we would bring Kareem in to work with our big men. One day we had a young guy that was doing drill work with Kareem out on our practice court. When he completed his workout, he came into the weight room, sweating profusely. Tim DiFrancesco said, "Looks like you got a good work out." Our player replied: "Yeah, Wilt worked me out really hard." Wilt Chamberlain, who died in 1999 at age 63, had been dead for six years.

I have always been a pretty insecure and serious guy, but my years working with the jokesters in the NBA helped teach me to laugh at myself and laugh a little each day.

CHAPTER 7

YOU CAN TELL A LOT ABOUT A PERSON BY THE WAY THEY TREAT SOMEONE THAT CAN DO NOTHING FOR THEM

Shortly after the Lakers drafted Ronny Turiaf in June 2005, I learned we had a problem with his heart. But I had no idea how serious a problem it was until I got a phone call from Dr. John Moe, the Lakers team physician. "*I'm not worried about Ronny dropping dead on the basketball court. I'm worried about Ronny dropping dead while walking down the street like, today.*" Dr. Moe said quoting the Stanford cardiac specialist who had examined Ronny at our request. That phone call was the start of a life-changing five-day episode that taught me a lot about human nature in general and Lakers' team owner Dr. Jerry Buss in particular.

Drafted in the second round, 37th overall - Ronny was near the bottom of the NBA food chain, one step above an undrafted free agent. Second rounders did not get guaranteed contracts as first-round picks did. Ronny knew he would have to prove during summer league play that he deserved an NBA contract.

And that's precisely what he had just done during four games in the summer league held every year after the draft. The 6-foot-9 native of Martinique and brand-new graduate of Gonzaga University had scored and stood his ground in the bruising battles under the boards. The coaching staff liked what they saw and decided to sign him to a two-year, $1 million contract. Now his long-time dream of making enough money to move his mother and four sisters out of a Parisian project was about to come true.

But there was one last hurdle to complete his improbable journey from Martinique to France to Gonzaga to the Lakers: even though he had already passed a physical exam at the NBA combine before the draft, he still had to pass our team physical. That was my rule, and there were no exceptions.

The NBA combine is a league sponsored three-day event where all the potential draftees gather to be measured and tested. Then they play against each other to show their skills with dozens of scouts, coaches and team execs watching their every move. The combine is held every year in Chicago. I did not attend, but we sent a Kerlan Jobe fellow to help our team physician examine and record the medical observations on the draftees.

Back in my trainer's office at the Lakers practice facility in El Segundo, I started going over the notes recorded by the fellow on Ronny Turiaf. That was when I first noticed a small notation at the bottom of the page, a notation so brief that it easily could have been missed: ENLR A/R. Studying it, I realized that it meant he had an enlarged aortic root, which is the main vessel pumping blood out of the heart. If your aortic root bursts you're dead before you hit the floor.

Players are put into one of three categories after their combine physical: pass, pass minus or fail. Less than five percent of the players fail their physical, and the vast majority are a straight pass, with a few pass-minuses.Ronny was one of those few classified as a pass minus, which typically means he's got a physical issue you need to keep an eye on. We had drafted him knowing this because the word from the combine doctors was that it was only a minor issue that would have to be checked yearly. His aortic root measured within normal limits and the enlargement had never even come up during his four years at Gonzaga. And he made the All-West Coast Conference first-team three times and was named the WCC Player of the Year after his senior season. The impression we got was that it was nothing serious, just something we needed to monitor annually. Certainly, nothing that would prevent a long and successful career if his skills were good enough to play in the league. Still, I knew the responsible thing to do was to send Ronny to Dr. Moe, who would take a closer look. None of us had been at the combine, so all we had to go on was the combine notes. I called Dr. Moe and said I'm looking at Ronny's transcript and apparently he has an enlarged aortic root. Moe asked me how big it was. I had no idea, it wasn't on the report, and if it were, it would have been beyond my scope to know what the numbers meant. He asked me to get to the bottom of it.

I hung up and immediately called Dr. John Hefron, the orthopedist for the Chicago Bulls. He was in charge of the combine's physical exams, so I asked him if he knew how large Ronny's aortic root was. He said he didn't know but would fax me the entire cardiology report. I, in turn, faxed it on to Dr. Moe.

Dr. Moe then faxed it on to Dr. Hattori at Apex Cardiology, located at Centinela Hospital in LA. He took a look and said this aortic root is big, all right, but is that because he's a big guy? Or is it too big even for a big guy? Dr. Hattori's entire team took a look, and now brains way above my pay grade were getting into this issue. The first group reaction was that this kind of problem is common with people who suffer from Marfan's Syndrome. Marfan's sufferers tend to dislocate joints very easily, and it's common to dislocate the lens of their eye. It affects the same kind of tissue that holds the aorta together, so their first thought was that he must have Marfans Syndrome. So let's send him to a Marfan's specialist at UCLA. But Marfan's tends to run in families, with a strong genetic component. We quickly learned there was no Marfan's in Ronny's family, so we knew that probably wasn't a correct diagnosis.

That was when we decided to send him to Stanford to be checked by a cardiac specialist. When we got the verdict from him – forget about playing basketball, Ronny was in mortal danger just walking down the street. There were plenty of tears to go around the trainer's room. I was devastated by the bad news. Not only was he not going to get the million-dollar contract that he had worked so hard for - the contract that would enable his family to move out of abject poverty. He would also have to undergo complicated surgery likely to cost a million dollars or more. And even if the operation was successful, there was no guarantee he would ever be able to play basketball again – amateur or pro.

Beyond that, the immediate problem was that Ronny needed the surgery as soon as possible, but he had no health insurance because he was in limbo: he had graduated from Gonzaga but hadn't yet signed a contract with the Lakers. He wasn't covered by the team's medical insurance. I had been around the NBA long enough to know the bottom line: he was on his own financially. I also knew that most teams would have quickly said good luck, go back to France with its socialized medicine, and see if the government will crack your chest open and pay for your million-dollar surgery. If he had been a high draft pick, they would have done almost anything to protect their asset. But he wasn't. He was a guy on the fringes of the league who in one tragic moment had gone from a potential asset to a definite liability.

I called General Manager Mitch Kupchak with the bad news. He said he would get back to me with a decision on how the team would proceed. I was doubtful there was going to be a good ending to this cliff-hanger drama. A couple of days later, Mitch called me and told me that Dr. Buss was going to take care of it. He was going to pay for Ronny's surgery and all his related medical and rehab expenses out of his own pocket. He felt that Ronny had become part of the Lakers family the moment that we drafted him, and it wasn't right to abandon him. Dr. Buss made that decision with no guarantee that Ronny would ever play for the Lakers. The projection was that the surgery would allow him to function without fear but probably would not enable him to play basketball again safely.

For years, I had heard that the way you can tell a person's character is by how they behave when they think no one is watching them. But that day, I learned there is an even better way to measure a person's character: by how they treat

88

someone who can do nothing for them. Dr. Buss was the living embodiment of Teddy Roosevelt's advice to speak softly but carry a big stick. He was not a self-promoter, and he always put the team and the players first. He commanded great respect within the Lakers organization just by his physical presence. Several times I had seen him walk into a practice session – a rare occurrence, but it happened – and everybody from coaches to players to ball boys picked up the pace without him saying a word. Everyone knew when the boss was in the house and acted accordingly. Not out of fear, but because they didn't want to disappoint him, big difference. Doing something so generous for Ronny that he was under no obligation to do just added to the respect everyone in the Lakers organization felt for Dr. Buss.

A couple of weeks later, Ronny underwent a six-hour open-heart surgery. Six months later he had recovered enough to sign a contract with the Lakers and play out the rest of the 2005-06 season. He played the next two seasons and even became a part-time starter on the 2007-08 team that went to the NBA Finals, where we lost to the Boston Celtics.

He played so well that season that the Golden State Warriors signed him to a four-year, $17 million contract. Now he not only had enough money to get his family out of the Paris projects, but he had enough to build them the dream home his mother had long hoped for.

Ronny went on to play for seven teams over 10 NBA seasons. And he never forgot that it was Dr. Buss who made it all possible. I know that because he has been back to visit many times, and we even shared our tears once again as we talked about those two most emotional and most important days in his life: the day we received the terrible news about him needing surgery, and the day we learned Dr. Buss was going to pay for everything. He told me Dr. Buss was the reason he set up the "Heart to Heart Foundation," which provides medical care to children who do not have health insurance and cannot afford the care they need.

"Dr. Buss did it for me when he didn't have to, and I wanted to pay it forward," he said. "I will never forget what he did."

Neither will I.

CHAPTER 8

TALENT: THE MOST OVERRATED THING IN LIFE

You can never have enough talent on your team. Still, talent is the most over-rated thing in sports and in life.

Thousands of leadership studies and books have been written by so-called management experts. But I saw first-hand that leadership starts from the top by someone that commands respect by their very presence, by their physical and mental stature.

In my 32-year tenure as the head athletic trainer with the Los Angeles Lakers, I survived 13 head coaches, but my eight rings were won with just two: Pat Riley and Phil Jackson.

So, what was it about these two men that could take alpha males with huge egos and personal agendas and get them to respect the position of the head coach and sacrifice a part of themselves for the good of the whole.

After Magic Johnson converted seropositive for HIV in 1991, the Lakers went down-hill pretty fast, and we needed to re-build. The only way you can improve a team is through trades, free agency, or the draft. If you're not at the top of the heap, you better be at the bottom. The worst place to be is in the middle.

If you are at the top, you have assets that you can trade, and you have a team that good free agents will want to come to, to win. If you have a bad team, you finish at the bottom, and you can improve through the draft. The worst place to be is in the middle because you are not bad enough to draft elite players and not good enough to have tradable assets or to attract free agents. You're destined to mediocrity.

The Lakers avoided mediocrity. For the next five years, we were drafting assets and rebuilding. We had a brilliant general manager in Jerry West. He was able to take those assets and through player development, trades and free agency he packed the Lakers with better talent. Still, as talented as we were, we could not seem to win a title or even make it to the Finals. Some of that talent included Shaquille O'Neal and Kobe Bryant who were there for three years before they finally won a championship.

So what was it that for three years with a more talented team we could not seem to win, but with the arrival of Phil Jackson we won 3 championships in a row, and we did it with less talent?

You can never have enough talent, but it's not always about the talent. It's what you do with the talent.

It's been well documented, that back in the mid-1990's we had a very talented player in Nick Van Exel that absolutely hated our head coach Del Harris -- to the point that they almost came to blows.

Del was a great guy and one of the smartest basketball minds I have ever been around. Nick was a young kid from Kenosha, Wisconsin that played for Bob Huggins at the University of Cincinnati who was known for his rough style of coaching. Nick had a bit of chip on his shoulder because he had dropped in the draft to 37th overall even though he had first-round talent. But underneath his tough-guy veneer was a good guy that ironically turned out to be a solid NBA assistant coach after his retirement as a player. Their feud finally came to a head one day when Del kicked him out of practice. They squared off, but before they actually fought Shaq got in between them to break it up.

I pulled Nick aside in the training room and told him: "Listen, you don't have to like your coach as a coach. You don't have to respect your coach as a coach. You don't have to like your coach as a person or even respect your coach as a person. But what you have to do is respect the position of head coach. As long as he is in that position, you must do it the way he wants it done. That's why he's getting paid. He was hired to call the shots. You were hired to do what he tells you to do. That's the way it works. If you are doing something other than what the coach wants you to do then in essence, you are acting as the player and the coach. Bill Russell won a championship acting as both player and coach with the Celtics in 1968 - and again in 1969. You are pretty good, but you're not Bill Russell."

I tried to help him understand that for a team to be successful, we must all be on the same page. I realized early in my career that I was paid to render an opinion. But if my superior wanted to do it differently than it became my job to prove that he was right and I was wrong. This is a recipe for not only success but long-term success. Not being on the same page will relegate you to mediocrity. When you rise above mediocrity, it becomes contagious. It spreads through your team, and there is a level of pride to be a part of that team that comes forth.

Phil Jackson arrived on the Lakers scene in 1999. He was a proven winner and was able to command that respect and get everyone to buy into what he wanted to do.

Phil didn't give motivational speeches. His feeling was that you were a professional athlete, and you should be self-motivated. He was good at getting everyone on the same page to accomplish the same mission -- which was to make each other better and be the best you could be every day. If you were headed in the wrong direction, he got you turned around and reminded you that the strength is with the pack. As a coach, he was willing to listen to different ideas, but once a decision was made, he was good at getting everyone to buy into the game plan. The 100% buy-in doesn't guarantee success. But I can ensure winning is impossible when people are going off in different directions and talking behind each other's backs.

94

We had talented players, but they needed structure, so he put in the triangle offense where everyone touched the ball. Everyone felt that they were a part of the team's success. The offense is featured around the center, and we had the best center in the game with Shaquille O'Neal. Every pass and cut had a purpose. The team was coached and coached well.

As much has been made about the Kobe/Shaq feud they were able to win three championships in a row simply because Phil came in and commanded respect and created structure.

It was not only the talent of Kobe and Shaq that carried us to a three-peat. Just as important, we were a team of high character with the likes of Derek Fisher, Rick Fox, Robert Horry, Brian Shaw, Horace Grant, Ron Harper, and AC Green.

We were a family, and sometimes you fight with your parents or siblings, but you never stop loving them or relying on them. That's what it was like for the Lakers team at that time. The players validated and relied on each other.

When I would look at technology, I looked for two things: validity and reliability. Validity means does it do what you say it does. Just because you say it, it doesn't make it so. It must be proven to be valid. Reliability means, does it do what you say it does consistently. You get on a scale, and it says you weigh 200 lbs. Then if you get back on within seconds, it should read the same weight. If it doesn't, then you do not have a reliable piece of equipment. To add a third variable, you may have a valid and reliable piece of equipment -- but is it practical?

We're talking about technology, but it can be the same with personnel. Do you have valid, reliable, and practical personnel? That's what Phil Jackson had. Reliable players that you could count on doing what they were asked to do.

Pat Riley had the same thing in the 1980's Showtime era. Sure,

Magic had 42 points, 15 rebounds, and 7 assists in the 1980 championship game vs. Philadelphia. But no one ever talks about Jamaal Wilkes' performance. Audiophiles always refer to George Harrison as the quiet Beatle. Well, Jamaal Wilkes was the quiet Laker. In that same championship game, Jamaal had 37 points and ten rebounds. John Wooden characterized him as the ideal player.

Magic and Kareem had Jamaal Wilkes, James Worthy (who was nicknamed Big Game James because the bigger the game, the bigger he played), Michael Cooper (who was the NBA defensive player of the year), Bob McAdoo, Mychal Thompson, and sharpshooter Byron Scott on the floor with them during Showtime. And what about AC Green, who has 3 Lakers championship rings and still owns the NBA iron-man record. Green played 1,192 consecutive games in his 16-year career. This is still an NBA record, and I think this record will stand forever because we are in an era where players don't play as long, and they will take a night off not because they're injured but because they are tired. AC Green was the epitome of reliability.

When a general manager puts a team together, there must be some young guys, some old guys and some guys in between. The GM and the coach are expecting a decent performance night in and night out from each player in the rotation. Some nights a player will outperform their talent level and other nights they will under-perform -- but most nights you know what you are going to get. It's not only what the GM relies on, but it's what he puts his reputation on the line for. If the player doesn't produce there are two casualties: the player's reputation and the general manager's standing. Imagine having a career that relies on banking on a professional athlete's future performance. How many athletes have you seen have a banner year in their free agency year only to bust going forward? It's a crapshoot as to what he's going to do next, and he and his agent may have you in a box: pay him big money or else lose his talent for nothing, or pay him big bucks and watch him lose interest once the checks start rolling in. Professional sports may be the epitome of capitalism, which is based on supply and demand. You may be the 6th ranked forward in the league, but if you are a free agent in a year when several teams need a forward, and there is a shortage of free-agent forwards that year, you may become the highest-paid free agent in the league.

No one was better at predicting validity, reliability, and practicality than Jerry West. He built the Showtime teams for Pat Riley and the three-peat teams for Phil Jackson. For Jerry, it was about more than just talent. He had a unique ability to look deep into the heart and soul of an individual player and figure out where he fits – or didn't fit – in the larger puzzle of the team.

You can never have enough talent on your team. But talent is still the most over-rated thing in sports and in life.

There was no greater example of this truism than when Jerry West traded Vlade Divac to the Charlotte Hornets for the rights to Kobe Bryant on draft day in 1996. Vlade had been drafted by West in 1989 and became one of the first European players to have a significant impact on the NBA. He was Mister Europa Player of the Year, made the NBA All-Rookie Team and was elected as one FIBA'S 50 greatest players before Kobe's 1996 draft. He was a proven asset and a future NBA Allstar when Jerry decided to trade him for a 17-year old kid straight out of high school. What did Jerry see that other general managers didn't?

Kobe was drafted with the 13th pick in the first round. There is nothing on the surface that jumps out at you when looking at Kobe Bryant as a professional basketball player. He's not particularly tall or particularly quick as compared to his NBA opponents. Kobe was a talented player, but what if I told you he was not the most talented. Why does Kobe have five rings and more talented players have none? Kobe Bryant has the heart of a champion because he did more with less.

Here's how he did it.

Kobe not only worked harder than anyone else. He worked with purpose.

He was not only more competitive than anyone else. If he lost, he used the loss as a learning experience to come back stronger.

He was mentally tougher than anyone else in the game by telling himself, "yes I can." He was so mentally tough he had himself waterboarded by some Navy Seals just to challenge himself. And lastly, he consistently put himself in a position to learn. He studied his profession until he became intellectually brilliant at it. At half time while his teammates came in the locker room to check their emails, texts, and tweets, Kobe was in my room with a lap-top reviewing film from the first half.

In the beginning, it wasn't all fun and games with Kobe. There was a lot of heartache and heartbreak. But in the end, there was heartfelt love and respect for the man. The heartbreak never deterred his resolve to succeed.

As I noted earlier, Kobe and Shaq were with the team for three years before they won a title in their fourth year together. I had my doubts about the team given the talent level we had and our inability to win in the playoffs. In 1996-1997, Kobe's first year, we lost in the conference semi-finals to the Jazz 4-1. In 1998, we were swept 4-0 by the Jazz in the conference finals. In 1999 we were swept in the conference semi-finals by the Spurs 4-0.

Still, there was never a doubt in Kobe's mind that glory was just around the corner. I don't remember what I said, but I made a critical comment to him about him in the gym one day. He turned around and said you'll see when I put 5 NBA Championship banners up there.

And that's precisely what he did. Kobe rose above his talent to the point that the characteristic that least contributed to his success was talent. He proved to me once and for all what I always suspected: Talent is the most over-rated thing in sports and in life.

CHAPTER 9

RESPECT YOUR OPPONENT

The first time I heard of the Art of War by Sun Tzu was from Coach Pat Riley. It is an ancient Chinese treatise that addresses military tactics and strategies. The first of its thirteen chapters is "The laying of plans."

Sun Tzu says: "victorious warriors win first and then go to war, while defeated warriors go to war first and seek to win." Coach Riley was the ultimate strategist. He looked at every aspect he could control to try and win before the game had begun.

By 1988 the Boston Celtics were no longer a threat to the Lakers, but there was a new bully on the block known as The Bad Boys, Detroit Pistons.

The Pistons were the doormat of the league up until 1981 when they drafted Isiah Thomas out of Indiana University. They still had a tough time getting past the Celtics, but by the mid-eighties, they had become legitimate contenders to dethrone the Boston Celtics in the eastern conference. In 1987 they played the Celtics to a 2-2 tie in the conference finals. They were on the verge of winning game five when Isiah Thomas threw an inbound pass that was stolen by Larry Bird who passed it to Dennis Johnson for a lay up and a win for the Celtics in the game's final seconds. The Pistons went on to win game six in Detroit but fell in game seven to the Celtics in the Boston Garden.

Days later the Celtics then showed up in Los Angeles to play the Lakers in the NBA finals. Along with the Celtics showing up, Isiah Thomas showed up as well. Off the court, Isiah and Magic cultivated a strong friendship. More and more, I began to see Isiah hanging around our team. After each of the 1987 finals games vs. the Celtics, I would see Isiah enter our locker room with the media. I thought it odd at the time, but later I realized why he had this desire to be around us. This was his friend Magic's fifth trip to the finals and Isiah was looking to gain every piece of knowledge that he could. What could he find out from his friend and his friend's team that he could use to lead the Pistons to a championship? He was doing what Sun Tzu called the laying of plans. The plans to compete for a championship.

It worked, in 1988 the Pistons made it to the finals to play the Los Angeles Lakers. We were playing for the coveted back to back; they were playing for their first championship in franchise history. Each game opened with Magic and Isiah kissing each other on the cheek at half court. Kissing aside, the series was nothing short of a brawl with the Pistons taking a 3-2 lead going into game six at the Forum.

In the third quarter, Isiah stepped on Michael Cooper's foot, which resulted in a third-degree ankle sprain. It was immediately evident to everyone watching the game that Isiah was hurt and hurt badly. I wanted to like Isiah because he was always respectful and cordial to me, but the Pistons were such a bunch of goons that a legit rivalry began which spawned a hate between the two franchises.

Like the rivalry with the Celtics, I realized you can respect your opponent while still hating them and that's what happened with the Pistons and especially Isiah Thomas. I have seen many ankle sprains throughout my career, and I can honestly say Isiah's ankle was as bad as I've ever seen. He finished game six with a career playoff high of 43 points, 25 of which he scored in the fourth quarter on one leg. The Pistons lost the game 103-102 on two last-second free throws by Kareem Abdul-Jabbar. Bill Laimbeer was charged with a controversial foul, known as "the phantom call." Leaving it all out on the floor Isiah and the Pistons came within seconds of winning their first NBA championship. Now they had to go back for a game seven, this time with their star point guard and leader severely injured.

After the game, Piston head athletic trainer and an all-time good guy, Mike Abdenour immediately went to work on trying to reduce the swelling on an already blown up ankle. The Pistons had a good relationship with the LA Raiders who invited Mike and Isiah to use their sports medicine facility. The next day Isiah limped into a press conference with a bandaged cheek courtesy of an elbow from Michael Cooper. He was wearing a Raiders T-shirt that read "real men wear black". He told the world if he could walk, he would play.

Game seven began with Isiah limping towards half court to swap kisses with Magic. The Pistons had a 5 point lead at half time with Isiah scoring 10 points. Barely able to walk let alone run Isiah played sparingly in the second half watching his team go down in a seventh game defeat to the back to back champion LA Lakers.

I have seen many brave performances in my career but the one that Isiah Thomas put on in the fourth quarter of game 6 of the 1988 NBA finals should stand as the gutsiest exhibition in the history of basketball.

It's no secret Isiah Thomas had a controversial career. Some people love him, some hate him, but there's no way you can't respect him as an opponent. I watched him walk into our locker room with eyes and ears open, hoping to gain whatever advantage he could while laying his plans to bring a championship banner to Detroit. He suffered defeat and severe injury during his quest, but eventually, he did what he sought out to do. In 1989 Isiah Thomas and the Bad Boy Pistons brought a championship to Detroit sweeping the Lakers 4-0 and defended their title to win the "back to back" in 1990.

CHAPTER 10:

DEFINING MOMENTS AND MOMENTS IN BETWEEN

We all have defining moments through our journey through life. The definition of a defining moment is a point in your life when you are forced to make a transformative decision that will change your behavior and perception of things going forward. We all have defining moments in our lives, but as we grow, we often forget the moments in between the defining moments.

Aristotle said the whole is greater than the sum of its parts. This became the basis of the Gestalt perspective in psychology, sometimes referred to as "the law of simplicity." Observing the whole will help make sense out of chaos and unity among outwardly separate parts and pieces of information. We don't always see the world as it is. We see it from our perspective of defining moments and all the moments in between.

When I reflect on my career, I've come to realize some things are at the forefront of memory and other things that I have to search for. One of my great regrets was not to have kept a journal. Everyone's life is a book or a story to tell. Keeping a journal keeps the parts recorded for posterity, so when it comes time to sum the parts they are at your fingertips. Here are the parts I remember, but I'm pretty sure I have forgotten more than I remember.

The first Lakers' defining moment I experienced was long before I was employed by them. It was 1970. I was 16 years old and visiting my friend Steve "Satch" Hagedus's house. The Lakers vs. Knicks finals game was on in his living room. The Hagedus family had a color TV, and I had never seen a game in color. My family never splurged on such things. In fact, my mom didn't get a color television until I was off to college. In those days if you opened a bank account, the bank gave you a gift that was commensurate with the amount of the deposit. I don't know how much she put in, but when I got home from college there was a color TV in the den and I know she wouldn't actually pay for such an extravagance. Along with bank ac-

105

count deposits, we used to collect S & H green stamps. When you would go to the grocery store, they would give you these green stamps that you put into a book. When the text was full, you traded it in for stuff. That's how we got our set of dishes, and my godmother got her Funk and Wagnalls set of encyclopedias.

Seeing a game in color was mesmerizing to me, especially a Lakers game because, in a league that home teams wore white, the Lakers wore gold. I had seen Knicks games on TV only in black and white but never the Lakers. These were days before live national broadcasting. I had seen Wilt Chamberlain play when he was with the Philadelphia 76ers because it was an east coast broadcast but never saw him play with the Lakers, much less in color. There was also Elgin Baylor, Gail Goodrich and of course the logo Jerry West.

I was a die-hard Knicks fan but who couldn't like the Lakers. They were LA, the west coast and where the Beach Boys lived, plus they wore gold at home which looked really cool on color TV. I never wavered in my fandom for the Knicks but the Lakers on that day became my second favorite team in the NBA.

We watched as Dave DeBusschere hit a 17-foot jump shot putting the Knicks up by two points with no time outs in the closing seconds of regulation. Jerry West then received the inbounds pass from Wilt Chamberlain with 3 seconds on the clock, he dribbled to his right twice and then launched a 60-foot shot that went in to tie the game and send it into overtime.

As a Knick fan, it was a devastating moment but also one of complete respect for Jerry West. The Knicks went on to win the game in overtime which put them up 2-1 in the series and gave them back home-court advantage. They eventually won game 7 in Madison Square Garden to give them their first championship and Jerry West's 7th finals series defeat. In his

14 year career, Jerry went to the finals nine times and won just one title in 1972.

Sitting in my friend's living room at 16 years old who would have thought that one day the man that hit the 60 ft shot would hire me and become not only my boss but also my friend and one of my mentors. On one occasion over many things we would discuss over the years, Jerry intimated to me that he wished he had never made that shot. Of all of the finals losses, he endured that was the one that he regrets the most. The 1970 Jerry West's 60 ft shot happened before the league instituted the 3 point shot. In today's NBA that shot would have won the game and quite possibly turned the tides of the series.

When I think of Jerry West, Diogenes comes to mind. Diogenes was a Greek philosopher that modeled himself after Heracles who thought virtue was action, not theory. As Greek lore goes, Diogenes was known for walking around in daylight with a lantern. When he was asked why are you walking around during the daytime with a lantern he replied I am looking for one honest man. Jerry West is the guy he was looking for; he's the most honest man I know. Beginning in 1984 Lakers defining moments became more personal to me because I was there — the first seat on the bench.

These are my most important single defining moments during my 32-year career - what I saw from the best seat in the house.

Going back to the 1985 final series vs. the Boston Celtics there was a moment when it was apparent the Lakers were finally going to beat their nemesis. With 1:02 on the clock in the 4th quarter Magic Johnson delivered a pass to Kareem Abdul-Jabbar on the baseline at least 15 ft from the rim. He pivoted and launched a vintage right-handed baseline sky hook over Robert Parish that gave the Lakers a 12 point lead with a minute to go icing the game and the series for the Lakers. My first championship! What they say is real - it never gets any better than the first time. I once heard Samuel Jackson, the famous actor, and Lakers fan say that you never feel any better from smoking crack than the first time you do it. That's the hook. You chase that high, but you never actually get there, but you keep chasing it. That's what championship basketball is like — chasing that high. Winning keeps you in the game, and it's insatiable. Losing destroys your will. Those athletes that say I just want to win one, and then I will retire, have never won one. Once you have won it, you want it again and again and again, but it never feels better than your first.

****

It's June of 1985, the Lakers just beat the Celtics for the first time, life is good in Lakers land, but some decisions need to be made. We have a future hall of fame player Bob McAdoo that is a free agent. Do we resign him and keep the family and the chemistry together or do we let him go? There are also salary cap consequences to consider.

McAdoo was drafted by the Buffalo Braves in 1972 with the second pick of the first round. He won Rookie of the Year honors and was a three-time consecutive scoring champ who once had 29 rebounds in a game, scored 40 or more points 56 times and scored 50 points in a playoff game and was the league's MVP in the 1974/75 season. But somehow he became persona non grata after playing for the Braves, Knicks, Celtics, Nets, and Pistons. When he played in Detroit, he somehow acquired the reputation as a malcontent and a malingerer.

My understanding of the malingerer part was explained to me by our team physician Dr. Robert Kerlan. Dr. Kerlan believed that McAdoo was misdiagnosed in Detroit with having a groin strain when, in fact, he had an abdominal tear. Abdominal tears are much more common in hockey and soccer than they are in basketball, but they do exist and are extremely difficult to rehab and often require surgery. When we played in Detroit, there was an extremely loud and nasty fan called Leon the Barber. He hated McAdoo and made sure everyone in the place knew it. He would start a chant: McAdoo McAdon't McAwill McAwon't. Everyone got a big chuckle out of it, but I know it hurt Bob, and we knew it was undeserved criticism from an angry fan that put a bull's eye on his back.

In today's NBA there is MRI and ultrasound to help diagnose soft tissue injuries which would have taken McAdoo off the hook but back then if a player knew he was hurt and the team put out there that he is ok, then that player is labeled as spoiled and soft. I for one can tell you McAdoo was neither of those things. He was a proud man and a competitor. It didn't make a difference what it was McAdoo would compete, and he always believed he could win. His teammates knew this and used to goad him into challenges.

This often happened in the stretching circle. As the story goes, Byron Scott and Michael Cooper were jawing at each other as to who would win a race in the hundred-yard dash only to see if McAdoo would chime in which he did. Through the conversation, he claimed he could beat them both in the 40 and the 100-yard dash. The challenge then went to tennis and billiards. Finally, bowling came up. McAdoo surprisingly said I don't bowl. Magic yells out, "Doo don't bowl." A proud McAdoo quickly responded, give me three weeks, and I'll bowl 300. A perfect game: 10 consecutive strikes. I'm sure in his own competitive mind he believed he could do it.

When he came to LA, he finally found a home with the Lakers. He was outspoken and wasn't afraid to rock the boat but was also loved by the other players and staff and fit perfectly into the chemistry of the team.

The situation was complicated. McAdoo helped the Lakers win two championships, but we were over the cap and the

109

Lakers option on him at 35 years old was in the vicinity of $980,000.00 which was a lot of money back then. By letting McAdoo go, it gave the team more options around the salary cap. I had just finished my first year with the team and was naive about such things. We just beat the Celtics, we're a family why would you break that up. Like I said it was much more complicated than that and that's why a guy like Jerry West was in the position he was in. He saw a bigger picture and was not afraid to pull the trigger, and that's what he did. We let McAdoo go to free agency.

The Lakers filled McAdoo's roster spot with Maurice Lucas by way of a trade with the Phoenix Suns. Lucas's nickname was the "Enforcer" which he earned while playing for the Portland Trailblazers when he elbowed Daryl Dawkins in the head during an NBA championship playoff game in 1977. Some say it turned the tides of the series allowing the Blazers to win the championship against the Philadelphia 76ers. He wasn't afraid of mixing it up in the paint, and there was still this feeling that we needed to beef it up in the middle to compete with the goon ball tactics of the Celtics.

At first, it looked as if the roster changes were going to work out. We got off to a 24 and three start and finished the season with the leagues best record of 62 and 20. But there was always this underlying negative energy that came with losing McAdoo. Seniority is a big thing in professional sports. Younger players are supposed to respect the stripes of a long-time veteran even if his best days are behind him. I used to joke that Pat Riley had what I called animal farm seniority after the book by George Orwell. All animals on the farm are created equal, but some are a little more equal than others.

We flew commercially in those days, and there were rarely enough first-class seats for everyone. In theory, seniority should rule as to who gets the seats but once again, it's animal farm security. Riley's rule was that the starters got the first-class seats even if there is a veteran with more years in the league. At the time AC Green was our starting power forward, and Lucas came off the bench. We had just drafted AC Green with the 23rd pick in the first round.

We gather at the American Airlines terminal at LAX for a road trip. In those days the name on the boarding pass rarely matched who was sitting in the seat. The season schedule would come out in July and as soon as it did our travel agent would book the flights not knowing who was going to be on the team. So often tickets would be booked under names of summer league players or players that were on the roster the season before that have since been traded or let go to free agency. I was the point person for seating on the plane. Everyone had a flying partner and a seat preference.

Kareem always sat in the first-row aisle, and the smallest person on the team would be put in the seat next to him. Behind him, Magic liked the window, and Michael Cooper sat next to him in the aisle. There was always some logic to the seating. For instance, James Worthy had a bad left knee so I would put him in an aisle seat on the side of the plane that he could stretch that leg out. I would do the same for Mitch Kupchak. Because none of the names matched with who was actually going to sit in that seat. I would handwrite their name on the boarding pass and then meet the players at the gate and hand them their boarding pass right before they stepped on the plane. I learned this the hard way when I used to give them their boarding pass curbside and then between the curb and the gate they would lose them.

AC Green was always early and got on the plane, taking his first-class seat as a starter. At some point, Maurice Lucas shows up, and I hand him his boarding pass. Without looking at it, he says thank you and gets on the plane. Within minutes he's back out in the terminal handing me back the boarding pass saying you gave me the wrong seat. I looked at it and said no, that's the right seat and handed it back to him. He said, but it's a coach seat. I said yes, we don't have enough first-class seats for this flight, so some players have to sit in the back. He says but AC Green is in his first year and I have seniority over him. I said yes in the league you do but not on this team other players also have seniority over him and they're in the back as well. He gets all puffed up towering over me, raising his voice. I said Luke I don't make the rules if you have an issue you need to talk to that guy over there, and I pointed to Pat Riley. Luke marched over there, and things got ugly quickly and publicly at the American Airlines gate. The argument culminated with Luke saying I have 12 years in the league doesn't that mean anything and Riley replying Luke we have good chemistry do you want to be the one to break that up? Luke repeated it; I have 12 years doesn't it mean anything and Riley finally saying no not on this team, it doesn't mean anything. Luke got the last word saying I'm going to the players association about this.

I gained great respect for Riley standing up to Luke the way he did, and the rest of the team backed Riley up. But truth be told Maurice Lucas had a point. He was not a bad guy; he was just a bad fit for this team. That single moment fractured the chemistry on the team. We were so good that our talent got us to the western conference finals, but there was always underlying negativity between Luke and his teammates. There was even a game in which Magic called a time out in the middle of the game. Time outs are called by coaches, not players. The only time a player calls a time out is for injury or if they are being tied up for a jump ball or falling out of bounds and will lose possession.

Riley turned to me on the bench and asked what's going on assuming someone is hurt. I say I don't know I didn't see anyone get hurt. The players walk to the bench for the time out, and before anyone can say anything Magic says to Riley, "take this mother fucker out of the game, I can't play with him." I had never seen anything like that before or since. That's bad chemistry, and it's the type of bad chemistry that comes back to haunt you when things start going bad. By the way and for the record Riley took Lucas out of the game.

It finally came to a head in the western conference finals. To get there, we blow through the San Antonio Spurs 3 -0 and the Dallas Mavericks 4 - 2. We now meet the underdog Houston Rockets with their twin towers Hakeem Olajuwon and Ralph Sampson.

The series will go down in history as one of the great upsets in the NBA. The Rockets win the series on our home floor four games to 1 with the final dagger coming from a turn around fall away jump shot with 2 seconds on the clock by Ralph Sampson. Maurice Lucas was no match for the Rockets big men. The Rockets went on to be beaten by the Celtics in the NBA finals 4 games to 2. The same Celtics team that we had beaten the year before with Bob McAdoo.

This was a defining moment for me because although I knew it was business and not personal, it was personal to me. We loved Bob McAdoo, and his loss affected our chemistry. We'll never know how the Lakers would have fared with McAdoo in the line up vs. the twin towers, but it had to be better than what we had.

After the series, we waived Maurice Lucas. McAdoo went on to play one more year in the NBA with the Philadelphia 76ers and then became the first real legit NBA superstar to play in the Euroleague where he won multiple championships and was named one of the 50 greatest Euroleague contributors. He was enshrined in the Naismith Memorial Basketball Hall of Fame in 2000. Bob McAdoo may be the most misunderstood player I ever worked with. One of the great injustices was him not being voted one of the top 50 NBA players of all time in 1997, during the 50th-anniversary celebration of the league. After his playing days were over, Pat Riley hired him as an assistant coach working primarily with their big men. As a coach, he helped the Miami Heat win three rings.

****

We begin the 1986/87 season without Bob McAdoo or Maurice Lucas. Kareem is aging, and we needed someone to give him back up minutes. After months of negotiations with the San Antonio Spurs, Jerry West pulls another defining moment for the Lakers franchise. He traded Frank Brickowski and Petur Gudmunsson, plus a number one pick in the 1987 draft and the number 2 pick in 1990 draft for center Mychal Thompson.

Thompson was the number one pick of the 1978 draft out of the University of Minnesota. In 1987 he was already 32 years old but was a chiseled 6' - 10" 235 lbs that could run the floor. He was exactly what the Lakers needed to defend Celtic Kevin McHale who was also out of the University of Minnesota. Thompson was so versatile he could spell Kareem at center or play beside him as power forward. The media buzz was so positive that when PR director Josh Rosenfeld asked the Spurs for Mychal's statistics, he also asked for his ring size.

The team went 65 - 17 and met the Celtics in the 1987 finals winning the championship in 6 games and finally putting an end to the Lakers/Celtics rivalry of the showtime era. Thompson was an integral cog in the wheel that went to the finals four out his five years with the team. With him, we won the coveted 1987/88 back to back, which had not been done in the NBA in 19 years.

****

1987 was a defining year because I learned the workplace is a constantly changing environment, and one needs to change with the times. That is what the Lakers did. Kareem was aging, and the trade to acquire Mychal Thompson to help Kareem in the frontcourt proved to be a brilliant move. Pat Riley changed the focus of the offense from Kareem to Magic and James Worthy.

Coach Riley adapted to the environment and made adjustments. Riley was so good at adjusting that when he was with the Lakers, we played a running game they called Showtime. Teams like Boston and Detroit played a much more physical game we called goon ball. Riley complained to the NBA and the officials all the time about the physicality of the eastern conference opponents. But when he became the coach of the NY Knicks, and he had Anthony Mason and Charles Oakley on his roster, two bruisers - he changed his style to goon ball because that was the personnel he had. Coach Riley studied personalities; he spoke to people with respect and never embarrassed anyone.

He had a philosophy that for criticism to work, you had to give four complements so if he called you out on a mistake you took it to heart. If you are critical of people all of the time or you are raising your voice all of the time then yelling becomes like talking so when you actually need to raise your voice to get someone's attention there is no place to go. Some coaches force their style on a group that is incapable of doing what they want them to do. It was also in 1987 that I learned the lesson of one needs to build on their strengths and work on their weaknesses. This was best exemplified in the greatest moment of the 1987 finals when Magic hit the baby sky hook to win game 4 against the Boston Celtics.

I bring this up because I see many players that have entered the league as a rookie and five years into their career they are doing the same things wrong with no improvement at all.

Magic took a lot of criticism when he first came into the league. First, they said he couldn't shoot, so he improved his shot. Then they said he had no range, so he improved his 3 point shot. He later put in the baby sky hook which won us a championship. We used to talk about him like he was detergent, he came back new and improved every year. He became better because he worked on his strengths while improving his weaknesses.

Next up was the challenge of winning the "back to back." While the Boston Celtics infamous front line of Larry Bird, Kevin McHale and Robert Parish aged quickly along with the tragic death of Len Bias the Lakers had a defining year in 1987 by improving and changing with the times.

Prior to the Lakers winning the back to back in 1987 and 1988 it had not been done since the Celtics did it in 1968 and 1969. So to say it was a defining moment for the franchise is an understatement.

The feat started after the celebratory parade through the streets of downtown Los Angeles that led back to a rally at the Forum parking lot in Inglewood. Tens of thousands of fans gathered to hear speeches starting with Chick Hearn and going all through the 12 + 2 + 1. Even I had an opportunity to address the crowd. Mychal Thompson bared his chest to the crowd only to be followed by Chick Hearn to do the same. It was surreal for me to say the least. Life couldn't get any better than this.

When it was Riley's turn to address the crowd, he did something that no one could have predicted. He publicly guaranteed to all Lakers fans that we would repeat. This was looked at as arrogance by the rest of the league. But in retrospect, it was the best thing he could have done. He set the stage in everyone's mind to work harder and be better. He went to each and every one of us and set individual as well as team goals. For a GPS to work, you must know two things: where you are and where you want to go. Riley was our GPS he knew where we were, where we wanted to go, and he had a plan to get us there. Winning the "back to back" was certainly a feat in those days. Many teams have done it since and there have even been a few three peats. We did it in 2000, 2001, 2002.

But for me, what was as great a feat as winning the "back to back," was we did it by winning 3 seven games series. Three times we faced elimination, and three times, we ended up winning. This defining moment taught me that no matter how difficult the situation, you never quit. No matter how much you want it to be over, you must never lose your resolve to win. No matter how hard things get, you must dig down deep and find a way for you to be the best you can be every single day of your life in sickness and in health.

I can honestly say that the pure agony of going through the 1988 NBA playoffs had a profound effect on me and how I handled personal adversity later in my life.

****

Sports, in general, are cyclical and the Lakers cycle had come to an end. It's no secret that the 2003 and 2004 seasons were both rife with organizational and locker room issues that eventually led to the demise of our three-year dynasty. With Phil and Shaq gone after the 2004 season, the Lakers needed to reload to become competitive again, but that doesn't happen overnight.

It wasn't until the 2007/08 season that the Lakers experienced their next defining moment with a midseason trade with the Memphis Grizzlies for Pau Gasol which quickly put us in contention to win a championship. Pau had already won rookie of the year honors and was a legitimate all-star. We went from struggling and grinding every night to winning the western conference. Kobe had an unselfish teammate that didn't need to take all of the credit but was willing to take the heat. Took it

117

he did. Pau was never treated well as a Laker, but he handled his time here with pride and dignity. We went to the Finals three times with Pau in 2008, 09 and 10. We lost to the Celtics in 2008 but came back in 2009 to beat the Orlando Magic and once again in 2010 to avenge our 2008 loss against the Celtics. Winning the 2010 Lakers/Celtics finals was a 7 game series that will probably cement Pau's place in the Hall of Fame.

Pau was a go-to guy that could score with either hand but sacrificed his game and bought into the triangle which required sharing the ball. With Pau, I learned that when you are part of a team, we should look at ourselves as being part of a puzzle. There are no extra pieces of the puzzle, you must figure out where you fit into the puzzle, and that's exactly what Pau did.

****

The following year I experienced my final defining Lakers moment in my 32-year career. In December of 2011 after a five-month lockout, the New Orleans Hornets did not have an owner and had been told by their superstar Chris Paul that he would not resign with the team for the next season. The Commisioner, David Stern was committed to keeping the team in New Orleans, especially after the Katrina disaster. Without a specific owner the team was owned by the NBA which was the 29 owners of the other teams, but the Hornets were told that they would be run autonomously by their current management which was GM Dell Demps and his staff. Demps engineered a three-team trade with the Hornets, Lakers, and Rockets. The Lakers would obtain the rights to Chris Paul while sending Lamar Odom to the Hornets and Pau Gasol to the Rockets. Dan Gilbert, the owner of the Cleveland Cavaliers, wrote a letter to David Stern calling the trade a travesty and demanded the trade be vetoed claiming it hurt the smaller market teams and strengthened the big market Lakers. Stern, in turn, vetoed the trade which meant the Lakers did not get Chris Paul, his decision also destroyed the Lakers team chemistry by telling two players you are no longer Lakers only to ask them to come back and play for a team that was willing to let them go. Pau Gasol and Lamar Odom were never psychologically the same after Stern nixed that deal.

It was the beginning of the end for Lamar. He demanded a trade to the Dallas Mavericks which ended in acrimony. He was then traded to the Los Angeles Clippers for one season followed by a stint in the Spanish league. Phil Jackson gave him his last opportunity with the New York Knicks that also didn't pan out.

Pau was never quite the same either. He felt betrayed by the team that he helped to 3 finals appearances two of which we had won. He was later rumored by Magic Johnson on ESPN that he was a possible trade option for Dwight Howard. He also did not fit into coach Mike D'Antoni's offense which moved him away from his place of strength in the low post and put him up to the elbow. Pau never publicly rocked the boat and did what he was asked, but deep down he was not happy, and when it came time to resign him as a free agent he refused to continue playing for the Lakers and instead signed with the Chicago Bulls.

After the Chris Paul fiasco, the 2011/12 playoffs resulted in a second-round bust to the OKC Thunder losing 4 games to 1. The following season we were swept 4-0 to the Spurs in the first round. The Lakers have not made a postseason appearance since. I can't help but think what if the defining moment of the Chris Paul trade was not vetoed where the Lakers would be today. Let's not forget Mitch Kupchak helped engineer that trade and it's my opinion that Mitch had never received the credit he deserved when things worked out and has always taken too much criticism for things when they didn't.

CHAPTER 11

SHAQ SAYS FOLLOW YOUR DREAMS

One beautiful day in the summer of 1993, I was walking down Manhattan Beach Boulevard in my adopted hometown of Manhattan Beach when I saw an incredible sight I will never forget: Shaquille O'Neal riding a moped. Seeing such a big man at 7-foot-1 and 325 pounds – on such a low-power, light-weight motorized bicycle was a hysterically funny image. He was acting like a clown and loving the attention, ultimately receiving stares of amazement from all in his path, including me. Shaq had just won NBA Rookie of the Year with the Orlando Magic, and he had made a significant impression on me when the Lakers played the Magic. I had never seen anyone with that combination of tall-timber size and cat-like agility. But we hadn't been introduced yet, so I didn't stop and talk with him.

That changed a year later in the summer of 1994 when director William Friedkin asked me if I would appear in the basketball film Blue Chips, starring Shaq. Friedkin was a huge Celtics fan and was personal friends with the Celtics equipment manager Wayne LeBeaux. Friedkin needed an athletic trainer for the film and thanks to Wayne I got the call.

I went to meet Billy at the studio, and as I left the building, a limo pulled up. A massive human being emerged and immediately yelled Garrrry Viiiiiti, as if we were old friends. I was not only pleasantly surprised that Shaq knew who I was but that he immediately made me feel like we had been friends all our lives. I had a great experience making the film.

From that moment on, I felt bonded with Shaq and rooted for him from afar. When the Magic made it to the 1995 NBA Finals, nobody rooted harder for him. Unfortunately, they got swept by the Houston Rockets. Little did I know that loss would soon have a profound effect on the Lakers and me.

A year later Shaq stunned the city of Orlando when he left and signed a $120 million free-agent contract with the Lakers. We had finally found our next superstar to help us add to the Lakers legacy of championships -- and he just happened to be my new friend Shaquille O'Neal. Being around him every day was great. A natural-born jokester and trickster with a personality as big as his physical frame, he filled the basketball court, the locker room, and the training room with life and laughter.

We had training camp in Hawaii, and by tradition, we had a team meal the night before our first practice so everyone could put a face with the names. Certain people were asked to speak. I introduced my staff and laid down some team and training rules as well as the training camp schedule. When it was Shaq's turn to speak, he walked up to the podium and said: "I am Shaq, and I am a mother fucking prolific scorer." Then he sat down. Point made and point taken.

At first, we got along great, and to this day, I'm still not sure when and why things started to go bad. But eventually, it got to the point that I hated being around him. Everything I initially loved about him – his man-child behavior, his goofy sense of humor, his all-around BIG KID personae – started to grate on me.

By the time Phil Jackson became the Lakers coach in the summer of 1999 Shaq and I fought all the time. Over the next three years, we won three straight NBA championships, and while there was a lot of glory to go around, there was also a lot of stress and conflict. The grind of an NBA season that starts in October and extends into June will do that.

Most mornings I could hear Shaq's big size-22 feet coming down the hall before I actually saw him. He would turn the corner of the training room on his way to the locker room and mumble: "Tell Phil, I ain't doing shit today." I think he thought I would follow him into the locker room and coddle him, asking, "Hey big fella, are you OK?" But I wouldn't do that. One morning he came back to the trainer's room and addressed me directly in his one-of-a-kind deep foghorn voice: "Tell Phil

I ain't practicing today." I stared back at him: "I'm not telling him… You tell him."

Shaq: "It's your job to tell him."
Me: "It would be my job if you're hurt or sick – and if you are hurt or sick you should have been here two hours ago when I opened the training room… But if you just don't want to practice, then you tell Phil."

Shaq glared down – way down -- at me as only a pissed-off Shaq can: "Just for that, I'm not talking to you for two weeks."

Shaq was a man of his word. For the next two weeks, he refused to talk to me. Of course, we still had to communicate. So, he would speak to other people in front of me in a way that I could hear what he was saying.

This was incredibly frustrating and childish, so one day when he did this in front of my staff, I said: "Don't buy into this bullshit. Tell him if he has something to say he needs to say it to me directly." My assistant did the right thing and passed my message along without adding any comments of his own.

Shaq reacted to his message instantly: "Just for that, I'm not talking to you either." And he kept that pledge too.

Trying to break the stalemate, I continued to talk to Shaq when I had to tell him something he needed to know or do. But it was a one-way street as he maintained his silent act. I kept on talking to him when necessary, but I never got a response. Next thing I know he turns up in the trainer's room holding a dry erase board he found in the weight room. Whenever I said something to him that required a response, he would silently point to one of the three phrases he had written on the dry erase board. And yet as mad as I was at Shaq, I never stopped loving him – he is, was, and always will be impossible to dislike -- and looking back there was an element of Shaq's playful, mischievous side in all this. But this crazy episode was also just the latest installment of our off-and-on conflict.

The core of my conflict with him was simple: Shaq, who had just been named Most Valuable Player of the NBA Finals each of the last three years, had the talent, size, skills, and agility to be the greatest basketball player of all time. Not one of the greatest – the greatest of all time. Or as the players say: The GOAT.

All he lacked was the nose-to-the-grindstone work ethic, the kind of fanatical, maniacal dedication to maximizing their talent that drove players like Kareem Abdul-Jabbar, Magic Johnson, Michael Jordan, Kobe Bryant and LeBron James to the pinnacle of their profession. Those guys didn't just want to be good – they wanted to be THE BEST!

I wanted Shaq to be the best, more than he wanted to be the best. And that was a festering problem. The blunt truth was that Shaq could have been – should have been - even greater than any of them, or indeed anyone else enshrined in the Naismith Memorial Basketball Hall of Fame in Springfield, Mass. He was content being a great player, the best center of his era, a force of nature that could dominate a game whenever he was in the mood to put in the extra effort. I understood that the game came easily to Shaq. He was a big man who dominated the paint whenever he wanted to. I came to believe that he made the game harder for himself because he was bored going down to take a position in the paint, receive the ball, turn around and score over his man. That's the easy way a big man scores in the paint: do all your hard work getting in position to score, and once you have position the scoring is easy. Too easy for Shaq.

So he would post up away from the basket and call for the ball, so he could show off his athleticism and try spin moves to get to the basket. Basically, he made the game harder than it needed to be. On top of that practice was boring for him, as it is for most big men. Shorter players tend to love the game of basketball. They can go to the gym all day long and work on their game. Most of them would play for free.

More prominent players, however, generally play not for the love of the game but because they are channeled into the game as kids just because they are big and athletic. Soon they learn that if they play a sport well, they are treated as unique and that feels good. Then they learn that girls like them because they play hoops. Then they realize that starring in basketball can lead to a college scholarship and eventually to a big-league contract for big-time money.

The game itself may be fun for them, but practicing the game is boring. There's only so many times you can do the Mikan drill – a drill for big men where they alternate left-handed and right-handed lay-ups, a drill named after George Mikan, the great center of the Minneapolis Lakers back in the 1950s.

Shaq hated to practice, but I felt he needed to practice to stay in shape and keep his weight down. He was also so big that he changed the game; the spacing on the floor was different because he took up so much space. If the team practiced without him, we were practicing things that were not going to happen in real games. Practice time was always a source of conflict for us. But one of our worst conflicts had nothing to do with basketball. It involved his obsession with wanting to be part of law-enforcement, an obsession so intense that one year he decided to go to the police academy. I understood the roots of his obsession: two of his uncles were police officers. And he was raised by his stepfather, who was an Army sergeant who taught him to respect authority and discipline. He had had an interest in law enforcement ever since he was a teen. But then one day he started taking it too far. He showed up in the training room and threw me up against the wall – in front of everyone – and ordered me in his best Officer Joe Friday voice to "spread 'em." And then he frisked me, pretending to look for weapons, drugs or whatever.

The first few times he did it it was cute and funny, so I played along with it. And of course, he was so much bigger than me that there was nothing I could do to stop him. I was at his mercy. But there came a day when I was busier than usual getting players ready for practice, and I just wasn't in the mood to be thrown up against the wall and frisked again. So when he reached across my face while throwing me up against the wall, I bit his hand. I felt like it was my only defense.

Shaq started yelling: "He's resisting arrest." And then he punched me. I saw it coming so I turned my body sideways, and he caught me flush on the back of my pelvis. Over the next couple of weeks, I had to get two injections from team physician Dr. Steve Lombardo just to be able to walk. But the Officer Shaq episode was just a side-show, and the ill feelings from our little "resisting arrest" confrontation soon went away along with the pain in my pelvis.

The conflict came to a head when we lost the 2004 NBA Finals to the Detroit Pistons. We had four Hall of Famers in our line-up – Shaq, Kobe, Karl Malone, and Gary Payton – and the Pistons had none. A couple of All-Stars, but no Hall of Famers. And yet they took the Finals, winning four games to our one. At the time, I put that crushing loss right on Shaq's big shoulders. He scored as well as he ever had but didn't have a lot of energy left over for defense and rebounding.

That following summer was a time of great turmoil for our team, and Shaq was traded to Miami a few weeks later. For all our intra-personal conflict, I was still sorry to see him go. He wasn't as dedicated to his craft as I would have liked, but he was definitely dedicated to making people laugh and feel good. As the years went by I missed that element of his personality more and more. I watched Shaq win a title in Miami, and then move on to stops in Phoenix, Cleveland, and Boston before retiring as one of the greatest centers to ever play the game. I also began to reflect on my frustration with his work ethic. I realized that I should not have tried so hard to impose my dream for him to be the GOAT if he didn't share that dream. I learned that sometimes you are forced to work with someone who is ultra-talented but doesn't see the world the same way you see it. The proper response is to do the best you can to get the most out of them and accept the rest the way it is.

Deep down, we never stopped loving each other, and we reconciled and hugged it out long before Shaq actually retired in 2011. But there came a night not too long after his retirement when I came full circle in my feelings about him.

I was invited to an event where he was given a humanitarian award for his work with young people. He was proud of the award because he has done great things for young people, and his generosity is beyond reproach. And I was just as proud of him as he was because I knew his work for kids was sincere and long-standing.

And so, at long last, it hit me: that award, and many others like it, was the fulfillment of HIS dream – to use his high-profile platform to reach out and help as many young people as possible to choose the right path in life. As many times as I thought he under-achieved on the basketball court, he had become an over-achiever in life.

I learned from Shaq that your dreams are your own dreams – they're not mine or anyone else's. And if you are not currently following your dreams, Shaq would tell you not to give up on them.

I still have an autographed Shaq jersey and a pair of his size-22 shoes. Every time I see them, I can't help but smile thinking of all the laughs we had along with the three championships we won together. Thank you, Shaq, for being you!

CHAPTER 12

YOGI SAID THE GAME IS 90% MENTAL, THE OTHER HALF IS PHYSICAL

Words are powerful things. But I learned the hard way that the mind-set behind certain words can be even more powerful than the word's surface meaning.

It's the fall of 1984, and we're in Washington DC to play the Washington Bullets, now called the Washington Wizards. The Bullets didn't play in DC as the Wizards do today. They played at the Cap Center in Landover, Maryland, which was a significant drive to get there and back for a shoot around on a game day.

We played in Philly the night before, so we bussed down after the game instead of flying out on the first commercial flight the next morning -- as was required for back-to-back games in those days. Our arrival time to the hotel was 1:00 am. Shoot around was scheduled for 10:00 am, which means the bus for shoot-around was at 9:15. Coach Pat Riley looks at me and says, "Find another gym for tomorrow morning's shoot around." He said he didn't want to go all the way out to Landover.

In my mind I'm saying to myself this is my first time here, I don't know how far the Cap Center is from the hotel. You've been here many times, and just now you are deciding you don't want to go all the way out there. I look at my watch and tell Pat it's 1:00 am. I can't find a gym for tomorrow morning at this hour. This is before cell phones, mind you. Pat looked at me and calmly said, "Well, have you tried?" Of course, I replied no...so he said: "Try." I checked into my hotel room... got on the phone and woke some people up who woke some other people up. The next morning we practiced at Georgetown University, and that's when I learned too often we say we can't when we can.

I never said can't again to Pat. In fact, I've tried to remove the word can't from my vocabulary. I also never wanted to get blindsided by a coach again. I tried to do two and three-step thinking. Trying to anticipate the land mines before I landed on them. I began keeping a scratchpad next to my nightstand and found myself waking up in the middle of the night to write things down that were in my subconscious. Things that Pat might ask me and I might not know the answer and possibly disappoint him.

I always tried to stay one step ahead of him, which was not easy to do given his intensity. I often over-explained things to Pat. I had so much respect for him and so wanted his approval that I would tell him why I made certain decisions. He would stop me before I could finish to tell me it's ok. I once replied, don't you want to know why? He said, "No, I trust you. The day I don't, you'll be gone".

I survived my time with Pat and 12 other coaches. I spent my entire 32-year career trying to manage on anticipation only to change the scratchpad to putting notes on my i-phone.

****

Sports Medicine is a big umbrella term that encompasses several disciplines. As an athletic trainer we are generally a jack of all sports medicine trades but a master of none. One of those areas I embraced was sports psychology. The can't and won't vs. the can and will are at the heart of the mental aspect of sports performance. As the great Yogi Berra said: "The game is 90% mental, the other half is physical."
I met Dr. Bill Parham in 1984 when I first joined the Lakers, and he was on staff at UCLA. I had taken sports psychology classes in graduate school and had thought for many years it would be our last frontier in sports. Bill and I often discussed the psychological aspects of sports, and I was eventually able to bring him on as the Sports Psychologist for the Lakers.

People often ask me about the physiological limits in sports to which I reply: you know the story about the kid that's pinned

131

under the car and the guy picks up the car to save the kid's life? We need to ask ourselves why was this person able to pick up the car under these extraordinary circumstances. The fact that he did it proves that we are physiologically capable of doing it. But why does it only occur under extraordinary circumstances? It's because of the psychological limits that we put on ourselves. We are all capable of extraordinary things, but we must break through the psychological limits that we have set for ourselves.

There's a reason why the big money people are in the big money positions. Everyone wants to win, but not everyone knows how to win. With the game on the line, you want the ball in the hands of players like Mr. Clutch Jerry West, Kareem Abdul-Jabbar, Magic Johnson or Kobe Bryant. They are not only capable of being in those positions -- they thrive on it. These are the "can" and "will" people of the world. They are willing to put their reputations on the line, and those reputations survive the test of time.

For most people, it doesn't come as easy. Professional sports are set up for failure, not success. That's why when we succeed; it's euphoric. Only one team can win the last game, and the rest are losers. This isn't youth sports where everyone gets a trophy for showing up and breathing. This is for all of the marbles, and only a few can win to experience the euphoria. Most fail and are depressed. I never scored a point, got an assist, or collected a rebound that led to a win or a loss. But I experienced the thrill of victory and the agony of defeat more than most. I can't imagine the agony of defeat when the defeat was because of your own failure. I saw first-hand the effect the game can have on an individual.

I applaud Adam Silver and the NBA Players Association for the strides they are making in mental health. This year my good friend and colleague Dr. Bill Parham has been appointed the inaugural director of mental health and wellness. Players like my most beloved Metta World Peace paved the way by opening up about his own mental health issues to the public. He auctioned off his 2010 championship ring to raise money for mental health awareness. In today's NBA, we have seen Keyon Dooling, Demar DeRozan, and Kevin Love putting themselves in front of the world to say, "I need help."

I worked in an era when it was difficult for a player to trust anyone with knowing they had mental health issues. Some players needed medication and wanted me to know about it and even carry it for them. If they had the courage and trust to tell you they would ask you not to let management, coaches, or teammates know. They were worried the information could be used against them for playing time and contract negotiations.

Other players never face their own issues but instead find a way to self-medicate through recreational drugs and alcohol. I had more than one player that fit that category, but there's one that truly broke my heart.

Orlando Woolridge was a great guy. He was an intelligent kid that went to the University of Notre Dame and was a gifted athlete. We signed him to a contract on the condition that he would get drug tested twice a week. We didn't have the drug policy and independent testing they have today. That meant I had to do the drug testing. I was provided with specimen bottles and postmarked boxes to mail to the lab for analysis. It can be an awkward relationship following a guy into the bathroom to have him pee in a cup. It wasn't something I signed up for, but I was a one-man show in those days and had to do a lot of things I didn't want to do.

Orlando was great about it, and I tried to put some humor into the situation. Every once in a while I would pee in one of the specimen jars and hide it in his luggage with a note: "If I have to handle your pee, you're going to handle some of mine." On Lakers' watch, he straightened his life up for a while. But after his playing career was over, there was none of the follow-up care he had while playing. Eventually, he gave in to his demons. I received a call from his ex-wife, Pat one day. She needed some advice regarding one of their children, who was a student-athlete. At the end of the conversation, I asked about his relationship with the kids to which she told me it did not exist. She told me the last she heard he was living under a bridge. It shook me up for several days.

I felt like I/we had failed him. He had family and friends on the team. He was well-liked and made millions of dollars. How could he end up a homeless guy living under a bridge? I sought out avenues to find him. I first contacted the NBA's drug enforcement program that had no knowledge, protocol, or means to find and help an ex-NBA player. I then went to the NBA players association and got much of the same. Their attitude was we exist for the current players and don't have the budget to help the retired guys that have lost their way. They advised me to go to the retired player's association. I thought for sure they would help, but the bottom line was no budget and no manpower. I was frustrated but had not given up.

To the NBA's credit, they have instituted a player development program that includes the rookie transition program and mandatory team awareness meetings that cover topics from money management to sex education. These team awareness meetings take place at the team's facility after practice, and players are subject to steep fines for not attending. The meetings are run by professionals in their fields and accompanied by one or more retired players.

One of these meetings was run by Dirk Minniefield. Dirk was a great player out of the University of Kentucky with a huge NBA upside but became known more for his drug habit than his basketball prowess. He is one of John Lucas's success stories. John was also a great NBA player but almost destroyed his career with drugs and alcohol. John entered the NBA drug rehabilitation program and came back to play four more years in the league. He started a much needed and respected aftercare care program which Dirk bought into and eventually became a drug counselor in the NBA's player development program.

I approached Dirk one day and told him about my experience trying to get our ex-player some help. There was really no program or avenue to help troubled players once they left the league. Dirk did something that will always have a special place in my heart. On his own time and money, he went and found Orlando literally living under a bridge and brought him to his mother's home in Louisiana. Once again he cleaned up, but his chronic drug use took its toll and damaged his heart -- which eventually gave out at age 52.

A more recent example of an ex-Laker dealing with his demons was Lamar Odom. Lamar was born in South Jamaica, Queens. His father was a disabled veteran with a heroin addiction and mostly absent from his life. He lost his mother, a corrections officer at Rikers Island to cancer when he was just 12 years old. His maternal grandmother raised him and four other children. She was a nurse and an inspiration returning to school to graduate from college at age 56. Eight years after losing his mother, his grandmother died when he turned 20 years old. Three years after losing his grandmother, he lost a child to SIDS. The tragedy train he was riding didn't end there. After he left the Lakers, his 24-year old cousin was murdered. The day after the funeral, Lamar was a passenger in a car that collided with a motorcycle that accidentally killed a 15-year-old pedestrian. Lamar has said himself that his life had been surrounded by death.

How does one cope with such catastrophe? Regardless of all the athletic success Lamar experienced, the effects of loss like that can be insidious. He was a national phenom in high school, leading the University of Rhode Island to their first Atlantic 10 title. He was the 4th overall pick in the 1999 draft by the Los Angeles Clippers. But underneath all of that success was an emotionally wounded human being. Lamar Odom is genuinely the nicest, most generous athlete I ever met. We acquired Lamar in the trade that sent Shaquille O'Neal to the Miami Heat. When he arrived, he told me he didn't believe loyalty existed in the NBA after the Heat signed him to a 6-year $63 million contract only to trade him after one season. It reminded me of a line from the Al Pacino football movie Any Given Sunday. Pacino was negotiating with the owner, and the line went something like this: "When I say it's family you say it's business and when I say it's business you say it's family."

Lamar learned that lesson again when the Lakers traded him to New Orleans for Chris Paul. Lamar had won the sixth Man of the Year award while a Laker. He was integral in us winning two championships. If you look at history, it was Lamar in at the end of games, not Andrew Bynum. I believe in Lamar's mind, he was finally living the dream. He had found a stable home and family with the Lakers only to experience loss once again.

As if it was written for a soap opera, David Stern rejected the trade and sent Lamar back to the Lakers. But he was hurt to his core and demanded a trade. Lamar was never the same again, finding himself at a Nevada brothel in a coma and near death. I believe the true test of one's character is what they do when things are going badly -- not when everything is going your way. But there's also a limit to what one can endure. Lamar has endured a lot, and to his credit, he is still trying to move forward.

We'll never know how many of us would react to what Lamar has survived. I know Vietnam vets that said they were surprised how their fellow combat brothers acted in battle and how they survived coming home as veterans of war. The ones you thought would be the heroes were not and vice versa. I learned that you can't judge a person until you have walked a mile in their shoes. Lamar didn't slip through the cracks. He crashed through the crevices. And there are other Lamar's out there. Where does the responsibility start and end as an employer, fellow employee, or friend? I continue to wonder what I/we could have done differently for Lamar.

Believe me, I'm no bleeding heart, but I also don't subscribe to the attitude of people that say they don't feel sorry for professional athletes that have everything and then self-implode. Mental health is a complicated issue that doesn't have one simple answer. These people are wired differently, either chemically or by their sometimes-dysfunctional childhood experiences. It's basically the luck of birth. I've always believed that the NBA is nothing more than a microcosm of society. Mental health is an issue that needs to be addressed and thanks to the people of today like Dr. Bill Parham, Metta World Peace, Keyon Dooling, Demar DeRozan, Kevin Love, Dirk Minniefield, and John Lucas we are moving in the right direction.

For those of us on the lucky side of the birth lottery, please find it in your heart to be appreciative and have empathy for the less fortunate. These people don't need to be beaten up.

They just need help

CHAPTER 13

IN TIMES OF STRESS TRAINING MUST KICK IN

Phil Jackson came to the Lakers organization sporting 6 championship rings and a history of working successfully with a bonafide superstar, Michael Jordan. Phil's ability to hoist banners afforded him instant respect and credibility with our team. Most coaches come in and have to earn that respect, but with Phil, it came with the job and the 12 million dollar salary. When management pays a coach that kind of money it's not so easy to get rid of him, if things start going wrong, it's easier to find someone else to blame. Players know that their agents know that so basically everyone knows who wears the daddy pants.

Phil had his own ideas about things, including how the training room should be run. Before Phil, I never had an issue with any coach about my training room. The Lakers training room had always been my turf and mine to run the way I saw fit. With Phil, the atmosphere was different. He thought the whole thing was his turf, and he had the rings to prove he knew better. We didn't always agree, but through our years together I think we got along well and more importantly we won 5 championships together.

For the first 13 years of my career, I was pretty much a one-man show going to the finals five times and winning three rings. In those days it was commonplace in professional sports to protect one's turf, and that included the athletic trainer. Things began to change around the league in the mid-'90s with teams hiring strength and conditioning coaches. We were a bit behind the curve of putting another person in the mix to help me because I was not ready to relinquish control. But by 1997, we hired our first coach to oversee the strength and conditioning of the team. For three years with our new strength and conditioning coach and a great deal of talent, we couldn't get to the finals, but when Phil came, he brought a championship staff with him.

One of those people was Chip Schaefer. Chip and I had a

long history. He was an undergrad at the University of Utah when I was the head grad assistant there. He later went on to become the head athletic trainer for the US Women's Ski Team. We kept in touch, and one day, Chip called me to tell me he was going to marry his college sweetheart and move to southern California. He asked if I knew of any job openings in the area. I hadn't heard of anything, but I had an idea. The National Athletic Trainers Association was making a big push to put full-time athletic trainers in high schools, so I approached Dr. Kerlan with the idea of having the Kerlan-Jobe Clinic hire a full-time athletic trainer and have him go around to local underserved high schools every week. Kerlan loved the idea and hired Chip.

Not too long after that, the head athletic trainers job opened at Loyola Marymount University. We often practiced at Loyola, and it was the site for the NBA Summer Pro League. I was good friends with the athletic director Brian Quinn and recommended Chip for the job. Brian hired Chip and later hired the famous ex-NBA championship coach Paul Westhead. Chip's network was expanding, and his love for basketball motivated him to go to the NBA. After three years of Division I college basketball experience under his belt and working the NBA Summer Pro League it was time for Chip to go to the big leagues, he just needed an opportunity, and the perfect one came along.

In 1990 the head athletic trainer for the Milwaukee Bucks, Jeff Snedecker had to leave his position because he had esophageal cancer. The Chicago Bulls head athletic trainer Mark Pfeil decided to move to Milwaukee opening the Bulls spot for Chip. Chip was well trained, grew up in Chicago, and waited for the perfect opportunity to knock and knock it did. The Bulls hired him and then went on to win six rings in eight years. When the Bulls dynasty fell apart, Chip got caught in the crossfire between General Manager Jerry Krause and Phil Jackson. Most of the time in the NBA, the head athletic trainer is like Switzerland, but some times you have to pick a side. Chip picked a side, and it cost him his job but not his career.

Because of his talent, relationship and loyalty Phil brought him to the Los Angeles Lakers along with his basketball coaching staff which included Tex Winter, Frank Hamblen, and Jim Cleamons. Phil retained longtime assistant Bill Bertka and me. Phil never told me, but I know he would have rather have had Chip than me as his head athletic trainer. I'm pretty sure the Lakers management told him I was off-limits. Chip joined the Lakers as my assistant, and we got along famously. I realized that Chip wasn't just another set of hands, but he was experienced at the highest level of championship basketball. He was not an addition to the staff that was new to the league and learning on the fly. It was the first time in my career that I had someone next to me that I could trust. It still took me a while to loosen the reigns but eventually I got there. I had done so much alone for so long, and I had to learn how to let go, and when I finally did, I learned that in times of stress, you prevent panic by being prepared.

Being prepared is being at the top of your game at all times. In the field of athletic training being at the top of your game comes from two places. First is experience; there is no substitute for experience. The longer you've been around, the more things you've seen that give you a perspective that goes beyond textbook learning. The second is being in tune with evidence-based practices. Staying cutting edge comes from continuing education in your field. Chip came to the Lakers with a wealth of experience and a cutting edge education. It's tough giving up control unless you have confidence in your staff. I finally had confidence in someone that I knew would be prepared.

With Phil Jackson at the helm that confidence also went to the basketball court. Phil was already an acclaimed coach, but he also surrounded himself with assistant coaches that were cutting edge with a wealth of experience. I saw no better example of this during the western conference finals in his first year with the team.

Before getting to the finals, we had to beat the Portland Trailblazers which resulted in a 7 game series. We were down 15 points with 10 and a half minutes to play in the 4th quarter. We clawed back and won by 5 capping the victory off with Kobe throwing an alley-oop pass to Shaq for possibly the most iconic dunk in history.

Down 15 points with 10 and a half to go, Phil did not panic nor did our team. This was when I learned that in crisis situations, your training needs to kick in. Phil had the team trained. We executed our defense, causing the Blazers to miss 13 consecutive shots while executing our offense outscoring them 29 to 9 to finish the game. Proper preparation and training in times of difficulty will make the difference between success or failure.

****

In October of 1997, I had a frustrating experience as an athletic trainer. Shaquille O'Neal suffered an abdominal strain on a spin move to the basket in a preseason game. I had treated and rehabbed several abdominal strains in prior years, but this one was slow to heal, and given Shaq's enormous frame, it put massive loads on his core. We did not have a full-time physical therapist at the time, so when the team was on the road, Shaq would do his physical therapy with the therapists in the Kerlan-Jobe building. With a combined effort, we treated Shaq for weeks with little improvement. Shaq, Dr. Lombardo, and I were all frustrated, and we knew we needed help. Although abdominal injuries occurred in basketball, they were much more common in soccer and hockey. We had a scheduled trip to play the Vancouver Grizzlies in British Columbia. The Grizzlies had the same team physician as the Vancouver Canucks hockey team, Dr. Ross Davidson. Dr. Lombardo had experience with abdominal injuries when he was the LA Kings team physician, so he called to confer with Ross about Shaq's abdominal issue. Ross referred us to a local physical therapist, Alex McKechnie.

While in Vancouver, we visited Alex. Alex is originally from Scotland with a heavy accent and pure white hair that earned him the nickname "the Silver Fox." He was extremely professional and told us exactly what we didn't want to hear but needed to hear.

We had to shut Shaq down, alter our rehab regimen and the timeline for return to play. We discussed the lumbo-pelvic-hip complex in a way that it was apparent this was Alex's wheelhouse, what he was known for, his passion. I wanted to learn more and more than anything I wanted what was best for Shaq which meant we needed Alex. Not long after, I was able to hire Alex to consult for us for 40 days per year. We would look at the Lakers' schedule and figure out how we could get the most bang for our buck. Sometimes he would meet us on the road and travel with the team. Other times it made more sense to bring him during a homestand.

Shaq got better, and I became a better athletic trainer being around Alex. In 2003, we were able to drag Alex away from his practice in Vancouver and hire him full time with the Lakers. His talent and experience went beyond the core training that helped Shaq return to play.

He is the best manual therapist I know, and he taught me many mobilization techniques that I used with great success. In addition to his talent, Alex knew how to fit in. He had a good presence in the training room that commanded respect. You got the best out of Alex whether you were a superstar or the last man on the roster scratching to stay in the league. Alex

143

and I were side by side for eight years, and I can honestly say I learned more about physical therapy from Alex McKechnie than any other individual I ever worked with.

During the Riley years, I was a one-man show, but the Jackson years with Chip Schaefer and Alex McKechnie gave me a different perspective on having a staff that compliments each other to achieve success. We never did daily meetings to go over what each of us was doing to each player on the roster. We were symbiotic in the training room. We knew who was doing what by seeing what they were doing. It wasn't a football team with 60 guys all over the place. There were only three places you could possibly be, and they were all one wall away from each other with windows: the training room, the weight room or the basketball court. We knew each other's skillset and protocols. All three of us had strong personalities and years of experience, but none of us were looking to take the sole credit for whatever success we had. The satisfaction was in the combined effort to achieve the common goal of putting the athlete in the best position to compete. For us, in the end, it was the athlete that deserved the credit. He was the one that actually had to go out there and do it, and we all knew that. I have very little respect for athletic trainers, therapists, or strength and conditioning coaches that take credit for an athlete's success, especially the success of a superstar. If you're so great, why can't you take the 15th man on the roster and make him a super star?

I know I received more credit than I deserved during my tenure with the Lakers and I would be remiss in not thanking my colleagues Chip Schaefer and Alex McKechnie. The Lakers were always prepared from the players to the coaches to the athletic training staff, and much of that credit should go to Chip and Alex. It was a privilege to have worked with both of them and an honor to call them my friends.

****

144

Being prepared and being comfortable in your job are two different things. Sometimes you can get so comfortable in your business that you don't see the obvious. You become part of the picture, and when you are in the picture, you can't see the picture. If you want great power, it comes with great responsibility, but sometimes it pays to ask other people what they think. Surround yourself with good people and value their opinions, but you must decide who and what you are and be that.

With my new staff, I was finally able to take myself out of the picture and look at the situation from the outside in. I was also able to do other things that I never had the time or opportunity to do. I was also transitioning in age difference with the players. When I broke in in 1984 Kareem Abdul-Jabbar, Jamaal Wilkes and Bob McAdoo were the only three players older than me. In 2000 I was old enough to be most of the player's father. It allowed me to do more mentoring. I requested a monitor in the locker room that showed the standings all day every day. When you are jockeying for a playoff spot, it needs to be paramount and in your face daily.

Along with the standings, the monitor showed the next five games on the schedule. There was also a message board in which I personally had control over. I would post information as to scheduled team awareness meetings or other pertinent calendar information. If there was nothing to post, I would use the space to put up a vocabulary word with a definition, and an example of a sentence with the word or I would put up a quote.

I once put up a quote that was directed at a specific player although he thought it was for everyone else but him. It was a Judy Garland quote: better to be a first-rate version of yourself than a second rate version of someone you want to be. This particular player was intelligent, talented, and athletic but not skilled. He could have controlled a game by playing smart and hard, but he tried to do things he couldn't do. He didn't last long with the Lakers and has worn out his welcome with several other teams as well.

Paraphrasing Portia Nelson, we will all come to a fork in the road in our lives and go down a road with a hole in it. You fall in the hole, but it's not your fault. You didn't know the hole was there. As you continue to grow, you will come to the same fork and go down the same road. This time you know the hole is there, so you tiptoe around the hole trying not to fall in. As you continue to grow, someday you will go down a different road - one without a hole in it.

I have watched this player continue to fall into the same hole. At some point, don't you ask yourself why do I keep falling into the same hole. One answer is that you continue to be rewarded for falling into the hole, meaning there is another team willing to pay you. If there is another team willing to pay you to do what you have been doing that is reinforcing the same behavior. For some, it's not until you have run out of options that you learn your lesson, unfortunately for many, it's too late.

Everything I have talked about is preparing for success. Preparation does not guarantee success, but coach John Wooden would say failure to prepare is preparing to fail.

CHAPTER 14:

GIVERS VS TAKERS

It's 1988 the Lakers win the "back to back," I have a one-year-old beautiful and healthy baby girl and a new contract. I didn't think life couldn't get any better and then it did. I received a call from the Lakers promotions director asking if I would like to give Hertz some of my tickets in exchange for a new car every month. I had four tickets, two nose bleeds and two in the lower bowl. If they were interested in the nose bleeds we had a deal. The Lakers were so popular during this showtime era that even the nose bleeds were of great value. At the time, I was the only athletic trainer in the league that didn't have a car deal or car allowance from the team. In fact, when I took the job, I had to buy a truck to haul the team's equipment around from practice site to practice site and the airport and back. I figured this was the Lakers' way of helping me out with an automobile. There were also a couple of players that got in on the deal. They played in L.A. but didn't live there, so it was easier for them to give up some tickets for a car instead of having their car shipped from home.

Before my new Hertz car, I had my work truck and a 1970 something Volvo sedan that was in mint condition. We lived in Manhattan Beach with a one-car garage and a tandem spot. Parking is a premium there, and now we had one car too many. The operations people at The Forum were a wonderful group of guys. They worked hard, and you could always rely on them for help whether it was a Lakers or personal issue that required tools or do it yourself advice. Erwin Beason was one of the operations guys that were taking the bus to work every day. The Volvo still had value and ran great, and I was on top of the world. So many things were going my way it was time to pay it forward, so I asked Erwin if he wanted my Volvo. I think he took the bus to my house and drove off with the Volvo and a pink slip. We started the season, I drove the truck to practices and the airport, but I drove my Hertz car to The Forum for games. It was near midnight as I was returning home from a game when I noticed a Manhattan Beach police car behind me. We lived off of the main drag in a cul de sac, so it was obvious he was tailing me. I was cautious not to speed or give him any reason to pull me over. As I approached the front of my home, the police car siren and warning lights went on. I looked in my rearview mirror and saw that the one police car had now turned into five police cars.

I stopped the car and rolled down the window to a command on a loudspeaker to put my hands out of the window where they can see them. I did as I was told with full confidence that this was some case of mistaken identity and we would get it straightened out. I told myself just not to do anything stupid. I then noticed they had their guns drawn as my wife came out of the front door to see why there was such a com- motion. They pointed a gun at her and told her to get back in the house. Her voiced cracked as she said that's my husband and disappeared behind the front door.

I was asked if I had reported the car stolen. I said no, I work for the Lakers and we have a car deal with Hertz. This is a Hertz car, and the registration is in the glove compartment. They told me to remain calm and to get out of the car. I said I have a seat belt on I have to reach inside to unbuckle myself, don't shoot me. They talked me through getting out of the car, and once I did, they put me on my knees and cuffed me behind my back in front of the whole neighborhood. One officer shined a light in my face and said hey I know this guy, he's the train- er for the Lakers. I said, thats what I have been trying to tell you. They retrieved the paperwork from the glove box, and the sergeant in charge told me the paperwork looked like it was in order, but the car had been reported stolen. He told them to un-cuff me and asked if we could go inside and straighten everything out.

Inside my living room with two police officers, I gave them the manager's name and explained that several of us had a pro- motional deal with Hertz rent a car at LAX. They called Hertz and were told no such deal exists, and the manager we were dealing with had no authority to make such a deal. The sergeant hung up and told me I just went from being a suspect to a victim.

An hour later, a tow truck showed up to take the car away. The whole thing was a ticket scam. Hertz rent a car at LAX had 30 thousand cars on their lot, and this one manager was not only trading with the Lakers, but he also had Kings tickets and Raiders tickets. He would then trade the tickets for other goods and services. In a word, it was embezzlement. He was subsequently arrested and charged. I'm not sure what became of him, but I went from having three vehicles at one time to one just like that. I guess this is what they mean when they say no good deed goes unpunished. I couldn't go back to Erwin and say I need my Volvo back, so I had to find another car.

The next morning we had to get someone to watch our baby while my wife drove me to work in the truck. The Hertz saga became the topic of discussion in the training room, not just about me, but we also had two players driving stolen cars as well. I was now in a pickle as a family of three with only a two-seat truck.

It never occurred to me to ask anyone for help. Athletic trainers don't ask for help. They are the helpers. To be an athletic trainer, you must be a giver. Most athletes are takers, so it's a good marriage. There's something in it for a giver to go with a taker. It makes them feel good to give, but for that to happen, the other person must take. There are obviously athletes that are exceptions, and an excellent example of this is James Worthy.

When practice ended, James walked into the training room and handed me the keys to a 1988 Jeep Wrangler. It was the car he was awarded for being voted the MVP of the 1988 NBA finals. He said, "I know you need another car with a back seat, keep it as long as you want". In my world, it was too generous, and I said James I can't accept that. He replied, I'm not doing anything special, I'm doing what normal people are supposed to do when someone needs a hand. I learned that day not to wait until someone asks for help. They may need your help but are incapable of asking for it. When you see someone down on their luck, you should offer a hand because they may not know how to ask for help even if they desperately need it.

James Worthy is a true southern gentleman. He grew up in Gastonia, North Carolina the youngest son of Erwin and Gladys. His dad was a Baptist minister that stressed faith and education. When the team would go to Charlotte, his mom would put on a spread for the whole team. I never experienced collard greens and sweet potato pie until Mrs. Worthy cooked for us, and once I tasted it, I couldn't help but go back for seconds. Mrs. Worthy also told James that he can always find 30 seconds to talk to a fan. I have never seen James ignore anyone that wanted an autograph or picture no matter the hurry. James taught me what true southern hospitality is. He is called "Big Game James" because the bigger the game, the better he played. We should call him "Big Heart James."

CHAPTER 15

GANGSTA

There were plenty of mob guys in New York City but growing up Italian 40 miles from Manhattan I can honestly say I never knew or even met anyone that knew someone in the mob. My family were hard-working immigrants that wanted to assimilate and erase the stereotypical uncle Guido wise guy image that was portrayed on TV. My mother was especially insulted by that image and was critical of me watching gangster shows and movies.

As a kid, I watched The Untouchables based on the memoirs of the famous FBI crime fighter Elliot Ness. The protagonist Ness was played by Robert Stack, who won an Emmy for the part. The setting was Chicago during prohibition with Al Capone as the main antagonist along with other members of the Italian mafia. All the bad guys were Italian, had last names that ended in a vowel, and spoke with accents.

My mother wasn't the only one upset by the depiction of Italian-Americans as gangsters. The show drew controversy from the Italian-American League to Combat Defamation. Protests were held which led to an agreement with Desi Arnez whose Desilu productions along with ABC issued a formal three-point manifesto:

There will be no more fictional hoodlums with Italians names in future productions.

There will be more stress on the law-enforcement role of Rico Rossi, an Italian member of the Untouchables who was Ness's right-hand man in the show.

There will be emphasis on the "formidable influence" on the Italian-American officials in reducing crime and an emphasis on the culture by Americans of Italian descent.

Since we didn't know anyone in the mob, I never really knew what my mother was talking about. They were just historic characters acting out fictional stories that provided entertainment for me. What I knew about the Italian mafia came from watching the Godfather movie, not anything in real life. To me, the term godfather was who your parents picked to christen you at baptism. It wasn't until I went to graduate school in Salt Lake City, Utah, that I experienced what mom was talking about. In 1979 being Italian was like being a unicorn in Utah. They hadn't seen one before, so what they knew of us was what they saw in the movies just like mom thought. There was an underlying assumption that if you were Italian, your family was connected to the mob. The first time I was asked if my family was in the mafia, I thought it was a joke. I quickly realized they weren't joking, which made it even more comical to me.

When I entered the NBA, it was more of the same. Italian was more like a race than a nationality. Magic Johnson once said to me, "you're not white, you're Italian," and I took it as a compliment. He would call me meatball or Italian sausage. I think there was a curiosity that if I knew people in the mob than I had stories of guys with names like Two Ton Tony or Vinny the Nose. The Italian gangster thing was always around for me, and there were always comments made and taken in jest. When James Worthy would leave the training room for the day, he would whisper in my ear, "leave the gun, take the cannoli," a line straight out of the Godfather movie after they whacked Pauli. Even Paulie became a locker room term. If we released a player, he became Paulie. If someone asked about the team waiving a player, other players would say, "oh Paulie, you won't see him no more."

There were always gangster jokes, but the fact is I never met a real gangster until I joined the Lakers. They were brought to me by our starting two-guard Byron Scott. Byron was no gangster, but he grew up in Inglewood, California not far from the Fabulous Forum. Inglewood was a tough neighborhood that on the surface didn't look so bad. Coming from back east,

154

my impression of bad was the South Bronx, Harlem, or Bed-ford-Stuyvesant. The race riots of the 1960s left these urban neighborhoods burned out and in ruins. Inglewood didn't have those scars but make no mistake about it, to survive in Inglewood you had to be tough, and Byron Scott was tough. He graduated from Morningside High School where he starred on their basketball team. The Lakers would occasionally practice at Morningside which was surrounded by a chainlink fence without one blade of grass on the campus. The fence was there to keep a specific element out, not the students in.

That element included gang members from the Bloods and the Crips. The history of these gangs is complicated, but I didn't know much about either one of them other than they were tough guys that wore red if you were a Blood and blue if you were a Crip. If you were neither, you avoided wearing those colors so as not to be mistaken as a member if you were in the wrong place at the wrong time. I was a Laker, so my colors were purple and gold. Byron grew up and was respected by both the Bloods and Crips. He was considered off-limits because he had another way out of the hood, basketball.

Byron told me one day he knew a few guys that had physical issues and asked if I would meet and give them some advice. I said sure bring them to the training room during off-hours. We picked a day and time, and four guys showed up. One individual walked in a very uneven manner and was the primary reason for them being there. As with any injury, you begin by obtaining a history of the incident. I was naive and didn't know these guys were gangsters, so I expected him to tell me he was in a car accident or he fell off a ladder at work.

He explained to me that he was recovering from being shot in the leg with an AK 47. As he lifted his pants leg, I could see this mangled lower extremity from the knee down. He further explained he lost about 8 inches of bone from the gunshot that required the trauma surgeons to graft back what they could. I

155

told him, I had never seen a high-velocity gunshot wound before and his issues were beyond my scope. When the other three heard I had never seen a gunshot wound before they asked me if I wanted to see theirs. They all had been shot at one time or another in their lives and wore their wounds like a badge of courage. It was a sobering moment for me. It hit me that the reality of growing up in the hood or the projects was more about survival than growing up. In later years I would often ask players if they knew anyone that was killed from gang violence, and it was the vast majority that knew more than one. This was Byron Scott's reality, and he wanted me to see it.

I knew Byron was tough and could fight, but this was a whole different perspective. It wasn't long after that meeting when he asked me to go to the gun range with him. I told him I had never shot a gun before. He said we're in Inglewood, it's about time you learn. We went to the range with a couple of Inglewood cops that worked Lakers games at the Forum. Byron had a duffle bag full of firearms. He pulled out a 9mm Glock for me. I remember it to be an almost surreal experience holding a weapon for the first time. I didn't feel empowered by it. I felt scared.

The guys trained me well, and I graduated from the 9mm to a 45 caliber. There wasn't much of a difference between the two handguns, but the next thing he pulled out of his bag was extraordinary. It was a Desert Eagle, the largest legal caliber allowed for a handgun in the United States. It was developed for use as a battlefield weapon rather than one for self-defense or casual use. It is the preferred handgun for the Israeli military. When Byron fired it for the first time, it was so loud everyone in the gun range stopped to find out what it was. It was a cannon with a handle. I was afraid of it and wondered why Byron had it, was he expecting a war? Byron didn't buy the Desert Eagle because he was preparing for war, but unbeknown to us one was coming. On March 3, 1991, a plumbing

salesman named George Holliday videoed Rodney King being brutally beaten by Los Angeles police officers after fleeing
and evading on California State Route 210. Holliday sent the
video to a local news station KTLA. The incident sparked out-
rage around the world. Four officers were charged with use of
excessive force. The next year three were acquitted while the
jury failed to reach a verdict on one charge for the fourth. Ten-
sions had been brewing throughout the trial, and within hours
of the acquittal, the 1992 Los Angeles Riots started. As the ri-
oting began, we were at the Forum playing game 3 of the first
round of the playoffs against the Portland Trailblazers. Less
than 4 miles away was the flashpoint of the riots at Florence
and Normandie. Down 0-2 going into game three we were in
the fight of our lives trying to compete for a continued playoff
run.

Little did we know just outside our doors Reginald Denny was
literally in a fight to stay alive. At 6:46 pm, Mr. Denny was
driving his red dump truck with 27 tons of sand to a plant in Inglewood. After entering the intersection at Normandie, he was
forced to stop, and a crowd of people surrounded him. He
was then pulled from his truck and brutally beaten in the
street. He sustained 91 fractures to his skull and a dislocated
eyeball. The whole scene was videoed by aerial photographer
Bob Tur and broadcasted around the world. For most people,
this was something shocking in a faraway place. For us, it was
happening next door to where we had to go to work.

When the game was over the Inglewood police put the team
on lockdown not allowing us to leave The Forum until they
thought it was safe. We were told to exit Inglewood to the south
away from the flashpoint of Florence and Normandie. Not
having seen the Reginald Denny video we were unaware just
how grave of a situation it was. By the time we got home, the
video was all over the news, and things started to sink in, not
just for me but for Byron Scott about me. The next morning we
showed up at the Forum for practice. Byron came straight to

me and said I know you saw what they did to Reginald Denny, you're not going to be him and he placed the 9mm Glock on my desk, the same one he taught me how to shoot. It was a blast of reality that this is really happening. The riots lasted for six days during which 63 people were killed, and 2,373 were injured. The NBA postponed and changed the venue for game 4 to the Thomas & Mack Center 300 miles away in Las Vegas which eliminated our home-court advantage. The Blazers took us out in game 4 and went on to lose in the finals against Michael Jordan and the Bulls.

A season that started with Magic Johnson announcing his retirement due to testing positive for HIV ended with the riots and a first-round bust in Las Vegas. When I think of the 1991/92 season, I don't think about the basketball. I think about the 9mm Glock on my desk and the man that put it there. Byron had a reputation as a tough player and a tough-love coach. He was a tough player, but as far as a coach, I would say it was more about discipline than tough love. I don't like using military terms like battles and wars when talking about sports. I think it trivializes what real war is like, but when it comes to Byron, if I were in a fox hole with him, I would know we had a better than fighting chance to survive and win.

Byron and I reunited in 2014 when the Lakers hired him as the head coach. We still talk about the events of the 1991/1992 season and the 9mm Glock. Of the thirteen coaches I had over the years, and as horrible as we were in my last two years, the most fun I had with a coach was with Byron Scott. I am honored to call him my friend, and I know he still has my back.

CHAPTER 16

THAT'S THAT WHITE BOY EDUCATION

Many people in society look at professional athletes as dumb jocks, but in my experience that has never been the case. I learned early on that there is a big difference between being dumb and being uneducated.

A great example of this was Kwame Brown. Kwame was the number one overall pick in the 2001 NBA draft by the Washington Wizards and was the first number one pick ever to be drafted straight out of high school. He was a high school phenom that entered the league with considerable hype and high expectations.

After three years with the Wizards, he was labeled an underachiever and traded to the Lakers in 2005. Kwame bounced around the league playing for seven teams in twelve years. He's considered a player that never reached his full potential. In Kwame's case, this was not a self-fulfilling prophecy. Kwame, regardless of the hand he was dealt, was determined to pull himself and his loved ones out of poverty. What he didn't know is he was set up for failure for a quick media headline. He faced extensive criticism and false reports that Michael Jordan made him cry and treated him like a child. That was both an insult to Kwame and Michael. It never happened! A 19-year-old kid fresh out of high school with no support system at all. How would you feel if that was your 19-year-old kid getting blasted on the front page of every sports publication?

To understand Kwame is to understand the disparity between black and white educational opportunities. Kwame was one of eight children growing up in a poor and abusive home. His father landed up in prison. Four of his brothers sold drugs and also went to prison. He had little opportunity at a young age for a solid education. But with all that riding against him, he found a way out. It wasn't just his basketball prowess that got Kwame out. It was his intelligence and hard work. By the time the Lakers acquired Kwame he was 40 lbs heavier than when drafted. This added weight led to poor movement efficiency and daily time in the Lakers training room for postural correction therapy. It was this time in the training room that I realized Kwame's thirst for knowledge. He often asked questions that led to deep cerebral conversations. One day I explained something to him that led to a line that will stick with me forever: "that's that white boy education." I knew the gap existed, but it became crystal clear that the absolute disparity between the educations of people of color and whites is much greater than I could have imagined.

Before people think that professional athletes are just a bunch of dumb jocks, maybe they should get their facts straight. In a league where roughly 75% of the players are black and expected to perform at the highest levels, they are offered the least educational opportunities growing up. How does this translate into functioning off the court? How does one with minimal educational opportunities deal with agents, sports executives, money managers, and the media? Are all these entities there to help? How would any young educated kid at 19 years old know what to do, let alone the likes of a Kwame Brown trying to navigate those shark-infested waters?

Kwame was one of many players I had that were bright young men, but by the luck or unluck of birth, they were born to lose. Many of them found a way to succeed despite their disadvantage. Unless you've walked a mile in their shoes, it's hard to understand. All you see is the athlete, and you never get to see the actual person behind the athlete. I was as close to these athletes as one could be, but I still don't know what it's like to be a young African American kid growing up in an underserved community.

Here's what I do know, and these are undeniable facts to help you understand what I am talking about:

Black students are often located in schools with higher concentrations of less qualified teachers, many of whom lack proper certifications and licensure requirements.

Research has shown a systemic bias toward lower expectations of black students by non-black teachers.

Students of color are often concentrated in schools with fewer resources. Schools with a student population of 90% or more of color spend on average $733 less per student than schools with 90% or more white students.

The average reading score for white students on the National Assessment of Educational Progress for 4th and 8th-grade exams was 26 points higher than black students.

These are just a few of the alarming and disheartening statistics that exist for the non-white community today.

Kwame's story is one close to my heart, but his arrival was not my first experience or thoughts about the educational disparity in our society.

After winning the NBA championship in 1985, I learned there was a tradition that the athletic trainer for the winning team picked up the dinner tab for the other athletic trainers in the league at the National Athletic Trainers Association annual convention. There was something about this tradition that didn't sit right with me. I've always had an issue with rich people giving other rich people gifts when there are so many that need so much.

As NBA athletic trainers, we weren't exactly breaking the bank, but we were making better money than our counterparts at the high school and college level. I thought maybe it would be better to take that dinner money and donate it to a good cause. I called my good friend Bill Schmidt for advice. Bill was the main man at Gatorade. Truth be told the orange Gatorade coolers and cups on the sidelines of every game was Bill's

162

brainchild. He is a giant in the field and has been recognized with numerous awards as a pioneer and innovator in sports marketing.

Bill suggested I create a foundation. With his help, we presented the concept to Rollin Mallernee, who was the legal counsel for the National Basketball Athletic Trainers Association (NBA-TA). We were quickly up and running, a charitable arm to the NBATA. I was the first president of the NBATA Foundation and had many ideas about what we could do as an organization to make the world a better place.

One of those ideas was to help fund the National Consortium for Academics and Sports (NCAS). The NCAS was an organization created by Richard Lapchik from Northeastern University. Richard was the son of Joe Lapchik: center for the Boston Celtics and head coach of St. John's University's basketball team. But what really set him apart was when he was the head coach of the New York Knicks in 1950 when he signed the first African American player, Nat "Sweetwater" Clifton to an NBA contract.

One of Richard's earliest memories at five years old was seeing an effigy of his father swinging from a tree across the street from his home along with picketers protesting the signing of a black player to a white team. At an early age, he became committed to using sports as a vehicle for social change and has been described as the "racial conscience of sports."
While I was in charge of the NBATA foundation, I am proud to say we helped fund the NCAS. Richard has done great work trying to be a resource for issues related to gender and race in sports. In 2001 Richard was accepted as an endowed chair at the University of Central Florida and has been operating from the sidelines there to issue grades for racial and gender diversity in sports. These are the NBA grades by the NCAS:

Overall grade: A **Racial hiring**: A+ **Gender hiring**: B

The NBA is doing its part, but these numbers reflect those that made it out of underserved communities through sports. For many young children, they see sports or drugs as the only option to succeed in life. This is what you get when there is no hope. Hope comes from educational opportunities.

Studies show that education is the primary vehicle for reducing poverty and closing the wealth gap between people of color and whites. The issue we have is that the people that need it the most receive the least and the people that already have the most are getting more.

It's not the lack of brainpower in our underserved communities; it's the lack of support and education. All children from K—12 should have an equal opportunity to learn on a level playing field. They're just kids. They didn't choose to be born into an underserved community. I'm not smart enough to know the answer, but I am smart enough to know that we have a problem, and it's a problem that we all need to take ownership of. What we are doing is not working!

There shouldn't be: "that's that white boy education" - there should just be good education for all.

SOURCE: U.S. Department of Education, Institute of Education Sciences, National Center for Education Statistics, National Assessment of Educational Progress (NAEP), 2015 Mathematics Assessment.

SOURCE: U.S. Department of Education Office for Civil Rights 1 Civil Rights Data Collection: Data Snapshot (Teacher Equity)
March 21, 2014 (revised July 3, 2014)

Ary Spatig-Amerikaner. Unequal Education - Federal Loophole Enables Lower Spending on Students of Color. Center for American Progress. August 2012; 4-16.

Gershenson, Seth, Stephen B. Holt, and Nicholas W. Papageorge. 2015. "Who Believes in Me? The Effect of Student-Teacher Demographic Match on Teacher Expectations." Upjohn Institute Working Paper 15-231. Kalamazoo, MI: W.E. Upjohn Institute for Employment Research. http://dx.doi.org/10.17848/wp15-231

CHAPTER 17

THE SHORT END
OF THE STICK

Of the thirteen coaches I survived, two got the short end of the stick. Usually being an NBA coach is a racket. You sign a multi-year contract for big money, get fired, and still get paid, then go off to another team and do it again. There are coaches actively coaching in the NBA right now that are still getting paid by former teams. It's the all-time scam in sports. Once you're in the club, you just keep getting recycled from team to team regardless of your win/loss record.

One of the all-time great assistant coaches was Frank Hamblen. Frank was born an Indiana Hoosier from Terre Haute in 1947 and played college basketball at Syracuse University and then started his career in the ABA as a scout/coach. Hamblen spent 42 years on the bench with the Rockets, Kings, Bucks, Bulls, and Lakers. He seemed to have been born a basketball savant, and when he passed away, he had been with seven championship teams.

To understand the short end of the stick, it must be put into perspective. The Lakers won the threepeat in 2000, 2001 and 2002. The 2002/2003 season was the beginning of an implosion, and we literally imploded in 2004.

Shaq delayed his toe surgery, which got us off to a slow start, and we didn't improve much when he returned. We were eliminated by the eventual NBA champion San Antonio Spurs in the second round of the western conference playoffs. But as a championship minded franchise, we knew the iron was still hot, and we needed to reload.

Now with the Spurs establishing themselves as champions, we knew we needed help in both the frontcourt and backcourt. Mitch Kupchak signs one of the best point guards in Gary Payton and maybe the all-time best power forward to ever play in Karl Malone. We are favored to win it all.

The Lakers go to the NBA finals against the underdog Detroit

Pistons and lose 4 games to 1. I think this comment by columnist Mark Heisler said it all:

"THAT SEASON WAS WHEN THE TORNADO COMES OFF THE HORIZON AND HITS YOU RIGHT BETWEEN THE EYES. THAT WAS ONE OF THE ALL-TIME WHACKED-OUT SEASONS FOR THE LAKERS, WHICH IS ONE OF THE ALL-TIME WHACKED-OUT FRANCHISES."

Things were coming apart at the seams. The Lakers publicly announced they would do whatever needed to be done to keep Kobe and do whatever they could to accommodate Shaq's trade request. When Shaq heard that, he did not show up for his exit interview, and the rest is history.

Phil left, we resigned Kobe, Karl retired, Shaq got traded to Miami, and Gary got traded to the Celtics. The first order of business for us was to hire a new coach but not just any coach. We needed a championship coach. Things were a bit different back then. It had been 20 years since the time I began with the Lakers to this juncture in 2004. In that time frame, there were only six coaches that had won a championship, and Rudy Tomjanovich had won two during those two decades.

To put things further in perspective: three of the six coaches; Bill Fitch, K.C. Jones and Chuck Daly had all retired. Pat Riley was with the Miami Heat, and Greg Popovich was with the San Antonio Spurs. The only proven championship winner out there was Rudy Tomjanovich.

Rudy coached the underdog Houston Rockets to back to back championships in 1994 and 1995, and he was available. The Lakers signed Tomjanovich to a five year 30 million dollar contract to replace Phil Jackson. Rudy was a players coach, a dichotomy in the sense he was extremely high energy but not in a controlling way. He is one of the most beloved individuals I've met in professional sports. Although we had never worked together somehow, we became friends when he was in Houston, so I was excited when we hired him.

We started training camp at the University of San Diego. I was never sure exactly when practice started or when it ended with Rudy. I don't say that to knock the guy, but Rudy was so consumed with the game that if he walked on the court during pre-practice and saw a player doing drill work he would drop everything to help that player and lose any sense of time. The same was true after practice. Practice is generally over with the team splitting up to shoot free throws and then a final salutation at the center circle to discuss where and when the team would meet next. If Rudy saw something that needed attention with a free throw shooter time meant nothing, he was zeroed in to help. Sometimes the rest of the team got tired of waiting for the final salutation so they would just walk out of the gym. That meant I was getting phone calls from players and staff alike about what was next on the team's schedule.

Rudy wanted to win so badly and was so high strung he nearly drove himself into the psych ward. Halfway through the season at 24 wins and 19 losses, Rudy T resigned due to mental and physical exhaustion, and that's when Frank got the short end of the stick.

This wasn't the first time Frank got the short end of the stick. He got it with the Milwaukee Bucks so he knew how it felt and he didn't like it. Del Harris did the same thing to him that Rudy did. Del was both the general manager and head coach of the Bucks in 1991. He inherited an aging team from Don Nelson, and although he tried to keep them competitive, it is evident that no matter what he did, they were not a playoff team. Del drove himself hard and had to resign as head coach due to health reasons. Frank took over with a record of 23 - 42 coming off an 0 - 3 road trip. The Bucks finished the season with 31 wins and 51 losses. Frank got caught in the middle of a power struggle between Del and Bucks owner Senator Herb

Kohl. He was fired, and Kohl hired Mike Dunleavy as the head coach.

Rudy T resigned on February 2, 2005, and Frank Hamblen took over as interim coach. The next day we lost to the San Antonio Spurs at home 91 to 103. We then hit the road starting the trip with four games in 5 nights and losing 3 out of 4. The 4th game was an 81 - 103 drubbing by the Detroit Pistons. After the loss, the team spent the night at the Townsend Hotel in Birmingham about 20 minutes from the Auburn Palace.

The moment I entered my room, the phone rang. It was our general manager Mitch Kupchak. He told me he needed my help to encourage Frank to agree to coach the team for the rest of the season. Frank had already expressed to me that he had no interest in doing so. His memory of how things went in Milwaukee under the same circumstances was not good. I told that to Mitch, and he said I know, but I've asked Frank to meet me in the lobby bar for food and drinks, and I need you to come down and encourage him to do it. I wondered who would coach if he wouldn't do it and Mitch said he would have to coach the team. I said I'll be right down. I love Mitch, but he's never coached before and would have died a thousand deaths with each loss, and a whole bunch of losses were on the horizon, so I knew I had to encourage Frank to finish the season.

Before I left my room, I called Alex McKechnie and recruited him to help with Frank. Alex and I had many dinners together on the road, and Frank would often join us. The routine was simple, go to our favorite restaurant in that city and head back to the lobby bar for a night cap. Going to the lobby bar in the NBA is like a ritual. It's where everyone in the travel party congregates before calling it a night and you also get to see who's coming and going with the players. Alex was much more social than me and always pressured me to have one more. Brian Shaw dubbed us "one more McKechnie and OK, Vitti." By the time the lobby bar closed, Frank had still not agreed to take over the team for the rest of the season. Mitch left it to Alex and me to take Frank out for last call at a neighborhood bar around the corner. We closed that place and headed back to the hotel. It was definitely past my bedtime, but Frank said he wanted us to come to his suite to open the minibar and watch game tape. Not something I wanted to do, but I had to take one for the team. We get to the room, and Frank gets a scotch, Alex gets an amaretto, and I had a small bottle of red wine. As Frank is rewinding the tape, he tells us there's a particular play he wanted us to see. He hits play, and to our surprise, there's a xxx scene on the big screen. We had a video tech that thought it was amusing to lace scouting tapes with snippets of porn to see if the players and coaches were actually watching all of his hard work. Frank said I got you guys. You can go now; I'll coach the team. The first pre game talk that he gave after agreeing to finish the season began like this. "Hey, fellas, I didn't want this fucken job!"

Frank Hamblen, one of the great basketball minds went 10 - 29 the rest of the season, 33 - 71 over his lifetime for a .317% win/loss percentage. He suffered through two horrible situations that he did not create but was asked to fix it. And that is what you call the short end of the stick. I lost a great friend when Frank passed away on September 30, 2017. He was 70 years old, may he rest in peace.

****

On October 15, 1983, the San Diego Clippers traded Swen Nater along with the rights to the 4th pick in the first round of the NBA draft to the Los Angeles Lakers for fan-favorite Norm Nixon. Norm was a tough, outspoken two time NBA champion. He was known as one of the Three Musketeers along with Magic Johnson and Michael Cooper. The rights to the 4th pick was Byron Scott who hailed from Inglewood, California just blocks from the Fabulous Forum. The trade created acrimony from within the Lakers locker room as well as the fan base. Jack Nicholson wore a black armband in Norm's honor, and Byron's new teammates treated him like a leper. He was a rookie, and the challenges that come with that were exacerbated by him taking Norm's place.

Byron Scott didn't trade Norm Nixon, Jerry West did, but Byron was the one that suffered. His new teammates were overly physical with him in practices and less than social off the court. Byron grew up in a tough neighborhood and was the last person that was going to be intimidated. He kept his mouth shut and did his job. The Lakers made it to the finals with him as a rookie, but he had a less than stellar performance on both ends of the floor and the team lost to the Celtics in a 7 game series. The loss was not Byron's fault, and he didn't blame anyone for his part other than himself and vowed he would come back better.

In 1984 I showed up as the new guy in the 12 + 2 + 1 cast of characters. The nucleus of a pro sports team is tough to break into without already making a name for yourself elsewhere. The core of this team were two-time champions. I came from Division I collegiate sports and the door mat of the league, the Utah Jazz. I knew I had to earn their confidence and respect, and I was prepared to do that, but there was one player that opened his heart and mind to what I had to offer as a human being and an athletic trainer.

That player was Byron Scott. Like me, he had yet to win over his teammates. Byron and I had to talk to someone, so it was natural that we would talk to each other. We took a crash course in trust and friendship. The trust issue came from the athletic training side. Byron was a fitness junkie and was open to strength training at a time when it wasn't popular in the NBA. He became the poster child of getting bigger, faster, and stronger without losing your shooting touch. His second year in the league while embracing a strength program he led the league in 3 point shooting percentage at .43% and became a hard nosed, tenacious defensive player.

Byron played ten years for the Lakers and was the starting two guard on three championship teams. He was a career average .48% shooter and was never acknowledged for having to defend the smaller quicker point guards in the league. Lakers point guard Magic Johnson was incapable of guarding the opposing team's points, so Byron was forced to defend the likes of Isiah Thomas and John Stockton. That's working overtime for a guy that's 6'4" 195lbs. He never complained about being put in that position, and he just accepted his role. After the Showtime era ended, Byron went on to play for the Indiana Pacers, Sacramento Kings, and the Vancouver Grizzlies. Byron was an extremely self-disciplined athlete that returned to the Lakers for the 1996 /97 season to mentor Kobe Bryant. He then went on to play the last year of his career in Greece for Panathinaikos.

Following his playing career, Byron was a natural to go into coaching. He was an assistant in Sacramento but soon went on to be the head coach in New Jersey taking the Nets to the NBA finals twice. He also coached the New Orleans Hornets and the Cleveland Cavaliers before the Lakers hired him in 2014.

Byron inherited a team in disarray that suffered the most losses in franchise history. Mike D'Antoni resigned, and Byron was asked to pick up the pieces. The culture of the Lakers was lost. All of the sweat, blood, and tears that went into the 16 championships since 1949 had disintegrated. We had our team dinner the night before training camp opened at Petros Kafe in El Segundo. Before the dinner, Byron and I had a very specific conversation about making this team understand that putting on the purple and gold was different than playing for other teams. It came with a certain responsibility and winning culture that was created by some of the greatest champions to play and coach the game. It fell on deaf ears, and we started the season 1 - 9 and ended up with 61 losses.

From my perspective, we didn't have players that were committed to defense, Kobe took too many shots, and we didn't shoot enough 3's in an era where the three-ball became king. Byron felt the 3 point shot did not win championships, but the analytics was telling us something else. Greg Popovich has said he hates the 3 point shot. He's even joked about having a 4 and 5 point shot. I don't like what it's done to the game. It's taken the game away from the basket. There are no more skilled players in the low post, and the mid-range jump shot has disappeared. The most important player on the floor is the stretch four. It's either a lay up or a three. The days of the in/out game are over. The three point shot was invented by Bill Sharman for the ABA. The idea was to get the smaller players more involved in scoring, which was great but now it's taken the big man out of the game unless he can shoot a three. I don't think Bill would like how it's evolved. Let us bring the game closer to the basket. How about if you get 1 point past the 3 point line, two from mid-range and 3 in the paint. At least at the AAU level to teach these kids some skills and footwork in the post.

Byron earned the reputation of a tough-love coach. It was more about discipline than tough love. The trick in the NBA is to try and figure out what makes a player tick and then get him to buy into what you are trying to do. He was demanding and hard on the players, and they weren't buying in. Part of the problem was we had an aging superstar that cost big money, but he was making the team big money. There was no way we could win with the roster we had, but fans wanted to see Kobe Bryant play before he retired. Most times in professional sports, there is an inverse relationship between being profitable and winning. A good basketball decision is generally not a good business decision, and a good business decision is not a good basketball decision. Donald Sterling was the

173

perfect example of this. He made a ton of money and never fielded a championship team. When it came time to spending money on a player, he let them go.

Now it was time for the Lakers to make money but they did it in a different way. Unlike Sterling, they forked over the big dough. They signed Kobe Bryant to a two year 48.5 million dollar contract that handcuffed the team. The Lakers did not give Byron Scott a winning team to coach, but they sure gave him a profitable one. We were the second most valuable team in the league behind the New York Knicks, but we were the most profitable mostly due to a 20-year television deal. Fans were tuning in to watch the Lakers play or should I say Kobe play and he put asses in seats. The Lakers gate receipts for Kobe's last year in 2016 were 99 million dollars.

Byron understood the situation. A professional sports team either sells winning or tries to sell hope. We had neither, so we sold Kobe. People came to see Kobe, so Byron put him on the floor and kept him on the floor. Kobe knew it too. I used to joke with him that he would take ten horrible shots and miss all 10 and Byron would keep him in the game. He would take the 11th shot equally as horrible, but it would go in, and the crowd would go crazy. It was understood this was Kobe's swan song and let him do whatever he wants out there. It wasn't uncommon for him to shoot us in a hole in the first quarter that we spent the rest of the game trying to crawl out of that hole.

Byron knew he had to fall on his sword and take one for the team. Get through the season and Kobe's retirement then we'll have money and assets to rebuild a team you can really coach. Byron did his part, but when the season was over the team did not renew his option and hired Luke Walton. Luke is a great guy who has worked hard and certainly deserves to be a head coach. I have no issues with that, but truth be told Byron got the short end of the stick. The world is not just and fair, and that's the way life is!

174

CHAPTER 18

THE QUADCHOTOMY OF THE NBA ATHLETIC TRAINER

One of the most common lines you will hear in professional sports is: "hey, I gotta guy." It doesn't matter what it is. Someone's gotta guy. If you need a car, a realtor, a tailor or an athletic trainer, someone's gotta guy. Every NBA GM has ten resumes on their desk to replace everyone in the organization. Every GM knows someone that's gotta a guy to replace you.

Jerry West became the general manager of the Los Angeles Lakers in 1982. In 1984 he hired me as the head athletic trainer. Sixteen years later in August of 2000 Jerry resigned and we went to camp without him. We were not better without him, but the fact is the team did not stop without Jerry. We played the next game. In October of 1991, Magic Johnson announced his retirement as an NBA player and we played the season without him. We were not better without Magic, but the fact remains the team did not stop without Magic. We played the next game.

I learned very early in my career that no one was indispensable. If we could go on without Jerry West or Magic Johnson, I wouldn't even be an afterthought. I knew I was dispensable, but it was great that I had people that didn't make me feel that way. From Jerry West to Pat Riley and later Mitch Kupchak I never felt like there was an ax hanging over my head. I felt a lot of pressure in my job, but it was self-inflicted because I wanted to be the best I could be.

My philosophy was if you did what was best for the player, you could never make a mistake. The team physicians, Dr. Robert Kerlan and Dr. Stephen Lombardo and Lakers management felt the same way. They were wonderful to me and never put me in a bad situation. By nature of the game, players are not always 100%, but it's a calculated risk to put a player on the floor. If a healthy player could get hurt an injured player is undoubtedly at higher risk, but it's a calculated risk. Unfortunately, not all athletic trainers in the league had the same management style behind them that I had. Many general managers and coaches ran their organizations with a big hammer forcing employees to look over their shoulder. There are still instances of harassment and constructive termination by forcing employees to quit rather than fire them. Abuse can be rampant in high-end sports, whether you are winning or losing.

The athletic trainer can be pulled in many different directions, what I call the quadchotomy of the NBA athletic trainer. The athletic trainer answers to both the GM and the head coach, which is fine if they are both on the same page, but what if they are not. It's the GM's job to put the team together for the head coach to coach. There are often divergent opinions about who the coach wants on the team and how the GM wants those players used. The athletic trainer maybe is hearing it from both sides, which could put that person in a very precarious position. There is a philosophy that you don't draft, trade or sign who the coach wants because if you fire the coach, you are stuck with who he leaves behind. I was fortunate to work for two class act general managers in Jerry West and Mitch Kupchak. I survived 13 coaches and too many players to count.

In each of those relationships, the athletic trainer must form a trust and a bond that is impossible to understand unless you have lived the life of one of those positions. The relationships between the head athletic trainer and GM, the head athletic trainer and the head coach, the head athletic trainer and the players are entirely different from one another, but all exist under the team umbrella for the head athletic trainer. A coach will never understand the bond between a GM and the head athletic trainer nor vice versa unless they have lived it. It's the same way for a player to understand the relationship between the head athletic trainer and the GM or the coach. Some players go on to be a GM or coach, so it clicks in later. Jerry West did all three. He played, coached, and then became the general manager. Maybe that was why he was so good to work for, and he taught those skills to Mitch Kupchak, who was an equally good leader.

The head athletic trainer has his office in the training room, and the training room traditionally is in between the locker room and the basketball court. As a result, he is in the midst of everything. The GM and the head coach usually have their offices elsewhere, often on the second floor. They come down for two hours to practice then go back to where they came from. As athletic trainers, we are not management or coaches or players, but we are in the middle of these three separate entities, and it's our job to connect the three. We are the eyes and ears for the GM and the head coach, but that doesn't mean you are a spy and run upstairs and tattle everything you see and hear.

Jerry West was an open door and an open ear for me. I knew I could trust him, and it worked like this. There were times I would tell him something, and he would ask me who. I would say I'm not telling you that. I'm just making you aware of it, and you'll have to trust me that it will work out. There were other times I would tell him who, what, when, and where. There were other times I would keep it to myself and say nothing. There was a trust that I would tell him what he needed to know and keep him out of what he didn't need to know. Mitch was trained by Jerry, and although he had his own way of doing things this philosophy continued, and till this day, we can rely on and trust each other.

I tried to have the same philosophy with my coaches, and for the most part, it worked. But by nature, most coaches are very controlling. They think they need to know everything and be involved in every decision, including the roster and staff. Sometimes the head coach inherits a staff, and almost always he inherits the athletic trainer. I can only remember one coach that challenged me on the who, what, when, and where. I would not give up the player, and he called me at home at mid-night wound up in a tizzy. I still would not give him up, and he just couldn't understand that. Of the thirteen he was the worst coach I worked with, and the team suffered with him at the helm.

The head athletic trainer and player relationship is another totally different animal. You can be friendly, but it's difficult to be their friend because you have to get them to do stuff they don't want to do. If you come off as a spy or rat, you will lose their respect. I saw and heard things on and off the court that were detrimental to the team. These are young kids with a lot of money and a lot of time on their hands, which is a bad combination that leads to bad decisions. I always liked the Dean Martin quote: "Good decisions come from experience and experience, well that comes from bad decisions." I would tell players do not put me in a position where I had to go to management about their behavior. I made it simple for them, they knew I would never lie to them, but I also made sure they knew I would never lie for them.

The fourth entity in the quadchotomy of the athletic trainer is the agent. When I first came to the NBA, I did not know any of the player's agents. When I retired in 2016, I knew them all, and they had my number on speed dial. If a player was injured in the game and I had to take him off the floor - back to the training room before I could get there my cell phone was ringing.

Most of the agents were good guys and only wanted what was best for their players, but some had their own agendas. The good ones could be quite helpful in talking sense into a player when needed. The ones with their own agendas often gave players bad advice that led to a bad image and a shortened career. I treated the agents as I did the players. I will never lie to you, but I will also never lie for you or your client. As a result, I think I retired with good head athletic trainer and agent relationships, but they certainly complicated things. I'm not saying having them around is a bad thing, it's just complicated when you keep adding more people into the decision making process. All chefs know; too many cooks spoil the soup.

The challenges of working as an NBA athletic trainer are four-fold; hence, the title of this chapter, "The Quadchotomy." It's not any different for most people. Yours may be a dichotomy or trichotomy. The fact is we are all pulled in different directions, and sometimes you may be torn by different entities that will try to affect your decisions. How does one make the right decision? I tried to follow the advice of the wisest man in history. His name is Soloman, and his counsel is known as the Book of Proverbs. Soloman said that "a good name is more desirable than great riches; to be esteemed is better than silver or gold. (Prov 22:1). The difficult decisions you make in life will determine your reputation, which will be your greatest asset and your legacy.

CHAPTER 19

PAT RILEY TOLD ME THE FUTURE IS WAITING

My first Lakers trip to Oakland to play the Golden State Warriors was when Dick D'Oliva was their head athletic trainer. He wore a championship ring from the 1975 Warriors team that had Hall of Famers Jamaal Wilkes and Rick Barry on their roster. Following Dick's tenure, Tom Abdenour took over. I already knew Tom from his days as the head athletic trainer at Weber State University in Ogden, Utah. I even shadowed him one day during football season in a student exchange program. I also knew Tom's brother Mike who was the head athletic trainer for the Detroit Pistons. Our teams had ferocious battles, but Mike was always the consummate professional, and even though we were on opposite sides, he never let it affect our friendship.

Tom is a social animal; he's warm and friendly and has a way of opening himself up and connecting with people. Not long after his arrival in Oakland, he brought Barry Weinberg, the head athletic trainer for the Oakland A's to one of our shoot arounds. Barry and I hit it off, and over the years we have become more like brothers than friends. Much like Tom, Barry has a way of networking people. Over the years with Barry, I became friendly with Tony LaRussa, Dennis Eckersly and Mark Maguire. I've had many dinners with them, and I can genuinely say they are all the class of baseball. But Barry's circle extends far beyond baseball.

He knows people in NASCAR, country music, Broadway, and professional golf, which is where this conversation is going. Barry is tight with Billy Andrade who is a PGA champion that now plays on the senior tour. I had the pleasure of meeting Billy soon after I retired when he invited me to play in his East Lake Invitational Golf Tournament. The East Lake Foundation has done great things in the underserved community of Atlanta, and I am happy to support it. It hosts it's Invitational in late September after the FedEx Cup, and it's a who's who of professional athletes and TV and movie celebrities. I've been able to play in it three times and the team I was assigned to even won it one year with little to no help from me.

At the end of October every year, Billy invites me to follow him to The Showdown at Sherwood Country Club. It's for the Invescso Championship which takes place in Thousand Oaks, California. In the last couple of years, I've driven up with an avid golfer friend of mine Tommy Barone. Working in VIP services for American Airlines for more than three decades, Tommy is no stranger to celebrity golfers, and he loves the game. We walk the course with Billy and have lunch in the clubhouse with the athletic trainers and physical therapists that take care of the golfers. The pro golfers get the same treatment as any professional athlete, but it's in a double-wide trailer that is converted into a training room.

The double-wide traverses the country out ahead of the tour, so the athletic trainers and therapists are waiting for the players as they arrive. The staff physical therapist is Paul (Doogie) Hospenthal and the athletic trainer is Kent Biggerstaff, a longtime athletic trainer for the Pittsburgh Pirates. We are all friends through Barry Weinberg, and we get together every year to support Billy Andrade.

Sherwood Country Club is a hop, skip and a jump from Malibu where one of my favorite people has a wonderful restaurant. Tra Di Noi is an Italian restaurant in the Malibu Country Mart. The owner is Tarcisio, born and raised in Rome with a fabulous smile and a heart of gold. We've been friends for 25 years dating back to when I first bought my Harley Davidson in 1993. On Sundays, in the offseason, we would ride the famous Mulholland Highway and PCH to stop for a 3-hour lunch and ride home. Tra Di Noi is frequented by the Hollywood and music industry set as well as wealthy athletes that have purchased homes in Malibu. One of those people is Pat Riley. Pat and I have run into each other there on more than one occasion. On this particular day, my friend Tommy Barone and

I were on our way back from following Billy Andrade. I called my wife Martha on the way home, and she said why don't you stop at Tra Di Noi and pick up food, so we don't have to cook, and we can relax and watch the Dodgers play game 3 of the 2018 World Series vs. the Boston Red Sox.

As I entered the restaurant, I saw Pat Riley at the corner table. I introduced Pat to Tommy, and we sat with him while we waited for our food to go. Pat treated Tommy like he knew him his whole life. Pat and I have been separated by time and geography since he left the Lakers in 1990. He first went to the broadcast booth and then to the New York Knicks and eventually ended up with the Miami Heat where he is till this day. When I see him it's never planned, we run into each other at the arena, an event or in Malibu. I take every opportunity to tell him how much he has meant to my career, and he mostly plays it down.

This day is no different. I started talking about the Lakers' past and present when he stops me and says, "why are you still talking about the Lakers? That's your past!" I was stunned at the comment. What do you mean? Why am I still talking about the Lakers? Well, how about beyond my family, it's been the main focus for more than half of my life. He then reaches into his pocket and pulls out a pack of what I thought were his business cards. It turned out to be a blue laminated card printed on both sides in bold black font. The front side states:

WARRIORS DON'T LIVE IN THE PAST
THE PAST IS DEAD
LIFE IS NOW AND THE FUTURE IS WAITING

I turn the card over, and the other side says:

ABSOLUTE RESPECT!

He tells me to keep it and think about it. I not only thought about it. I obsessed about thinking about it. I was confused. Since my retirement, I have been doing keynote speeches both in the US and abroad, and I'm writing this book. Both are based on the past and the lessons I learned from the past. If we don't recognize the past, aren't we destined to making the same mistakes in the future? I say to myself, doesn't the great coach, speaker, and philosopher Pat Riley know that?

Of course, he does, I have great respect for Pat, and I believe he's right when he says one should not live in the past. I would say dwell on the past. When your identity is tied to who you are or what you were, it's easy to lose a sense of yourself, and it's hard to reinvent yourself, which was Pat's message to me.

Working in professional sports is like working in an alternate reality. It's tough to distinguish who your real friends are. When I first got the job, family, and old friends came out of the wood-work. People I hadn't heard from for years all of a sudden were knocking on my door. It's not uncommon to be treated differently. You go to the front of the line, not because of who you are, and it's because of what you do for a living. I was often introduced to people who blew me off at the introduction only to find out later what I did and then would end up in my back pocket trying to get to know me. I was often introduced as Gary Vitti, the head athletic trainer of the Lakers. Are other people introduced by what they do for a living? When that would happen, I would remind myself that being the head ath-letic trainer was what I did it wasn't who I was. I was Gary Vitti, the son of Mario and Sylvia, brother to Dolores and Carol, husband to Chris (may she rest in peace), husband to Martha, father to Rachel, Emilia, grandfather to Cole and a good friend to a few.

After a great deal of reflection on Pat's advice to live in the future it occurred to me that I'm retired, but Pat is still on the job. Professional sports are all about the future. You're only as good as your last game, and only one team can win the final game of the season. When I was working, I lived in the present and a lot in the future i.e., getting ready for the next game. I was always looking at the next game, the next week, the next month. You have no control over the schedule. That is made up by the NBA, so you really don't have a life, you have a schedule, and you do the best you can to live your work and personal life based on it. Even bringing players back from injury is based on the schedule. If a player has been out for a while, you want to put him in a position to transition his come back with the best possible outcome. This could be effected by the team or player that he would have to face upon his return. It could be effected by the number of games played that week.

Some times we play four games in 5 nights or 5 games in 7 nights. A player may be ready to return to play but maybe not that ready. There are times that we may have 2 or 3 or 4 days in a row without a game. Sometimes it pays to take one more game off to buy four more days of rehab. It's an inexact science that is complicated. Today the teams are helped by analytics, but in those days it was often intuition derived from years of experience.

People would look at the NBA schedule and say this is brutal, how do you guys do it? The answer is, I don't know. You just do it! You know what needs to be done, so you get up every morning and do it. The job took so much out of you that you rarely had a moment to smell the roses. When I retired, I finally had a chance to look back at all the good and all the bad, all the titles and all the tears.

I am no longer Gary Vitti, the head athletic trainer for the Lakers. I miss the camaraderie, but I don't miss the job, the grind. I don't live in the past, but I am a product of the sum of my parts, and some of those parts are my past experiences. When you retire from professional sports, and you are no longer identified with being a part of the team, you indeed find out who your friends are. Some people that you carried along the way no longer have use for you and show no gratitude for what you did for them. You may also be surprised to find out how much you meant to others.

In the end, there are some great memories and a few relationships that will stand the test of time. Pat's right, we should celebrate the past but not live in it, the future is waiting.

CHAPTER 20

HOW TO SPOT FAKE NEWS

My first training camp was held at the College of the Desert in Palm Springs. At one end of the court, there was an elevated stage where the media were allowed to view practice. This area was reserved mostly for the beat writers. These were the writers that follow one team day after day. They become invested in their relationships with their sources, and they are on a deadline. When the team Is playing games, the beat writers have plenty to write about, but on off days it's a bit harder to come up with content.

This is when you read stories about the athletic trainer or some other position that is not the head coach or a player. Our stories are filler during the off days. Since we were in a training camp and not playing games yet, the beat writers were looking for something to write about. Being the new guy on the block, I was a story on one of these days. I didn't think much of it if a writer asked me a question I would answer it. To me it was no big deal but when I looked over at Pat Riley and PR director Josh Rosenfeld I knew something was up. They saw me talking to the press, and there was a look of impending doom on their faces. They both corralled me, and the message was clear. They are not your friends, be careful what you say and nothing is off the record.

Even though that advice was always in the back of my mind, I did become friends with many members of the media. For the most part, they treated me fairly and made me out to be more significant than I was. I'm sure that had a lot to do with being with a big market team like the Lakers. John Black became our PR director after Josh and also went out of his way to promote me whenever he could. Talking to the press changed in the early '90s. Now athletic trainers are only allowed to speak to the media under certain circumstances that are determined by the PR director.

The PR director is another one of these unappreciated positions in the NBA. They lie somewhere between the team and

management. They have to decide what information to dis-
seminate to the press for public consumption. There is a philosophy that the media sells the game, so it's important to give
them information to bring the fans into the inner circle. There
is also a philosophy that the game should sell itself, and there
are things that the fans shouldn't hear or see. The PR director
Is always walking this tightrope. Players and coaches think
the PR director gives up too much and the media thinks the
PR director is keeping information from them, so neither side
is ever pleased with the PR director. It's another thankless
position in sports, but it's one that allows you to be part of the
game. I was lucky to have Josh and John. They were both the
epitome of professionalism and did what they thought was
right for the team.

The media in sports has changed drastically over the last three
decades. The NBA has opened up the huddle and locker room
to cameras and microphones. Players, coaches and even myself have been wired for games. I once found a microphone
under my seat in an arena on the road. I told Pat Riley about
it, and he said get rid of it, so I pulled out my scissors and cut
the wire that led to it. That was a bad idea; the audio guy for
the other team lost his mind. He was ready to fight about it
until John Black intervened. We eventually agreed that it was
inappropriate on his part to put the microphone there and it
was inappropriate on my part to cut the wire. He was right; I
should have just removed it.

When the Lakers returned to that arena the audio guy, and
I would see each other from afar and laugh about the incident. Now there are microphones everywhere. It's hard to be
part of the huddle during a time out because you need to get
out of the way of the different camera people and the ones
holding a boom mike over everyone's head. Rather than fight
for a spot to hear what was going on in the huddle, I eventually surrendered my position during timeouts. I would miss what
was said in the huddle, but life with the camera people got

much easier. Courtside photography has changed drastically, as well. The famous sports photographers Andy Bernstein and Lauri Shepler used to have one or two manual cameras. Andy now has a minimum of 10 during a game. The new cameras are digitized, automated, and triggered by radio waves. When he would go on the road with us, he had so much equipment; he traveled with his own dollies.

But the thing that has probably changed sports journalism the most is the internet. Newspapers are going out of business, and the cost of distribution has practically disappeared because of the world wide web. Stories are more and more being dictated by social media. A journalist can follow what's trending on twitter and facebook and jump on that reporting bandwagon. Anyone can make themselves a media outlet using the internet, but how do you know what's real and what's fake news. The days of old fashion journalism with fact-checking and editors as gatekeepers of information are almost gone. Now the goal is speed over accuracy and the number of clicks on a site. There are algorithms and social bots that manipulate what and how much content is posted on the net. Some trolls open twitter accounts that appear to be the accounts of a credible journalist. The public believes they are reading a tweet from one of their favorite sources when, in fact, it's an imposter.

I do know some journalists with solid principles and standards. They hold the codes and canons of journalism to the highest degree, but journalistic integrity as a whole has suffered over my career, and fans should know that. I was once in a situation in the lobby bar of the Four Seasons Hotel in Boston after a Lakers/Celtics game. Someone very high up in Lakers' hierarchy was very drunk and saying things in front of one of our beat writers. These comments were way out of line, especially coming from this individual. I tried to run interference but couldn't, and the toothpaste was already out of the tube. As we parted, I asked the writer what he was going to do with what was said. He said he would never print what he heard under those circumstances. He felt the acquisition of the information while the source was under the influence was unethical. I gained tremendous respect for that individual at that moment, and we are close friends today. Not everyone out there operates at that level of integrity.

Much of the fake news is accepted as fact due to a manipulation strategy based on cognitive bias. The short definition of cognitive bias is a flaw in reasoning based on your inner preferences. It is a way for human beings to take short cuts to absorb information and make quick decisions. There is so much on the information highway that we suffer from information overload. Cognitive bias is our brain's built-in mechanism to deal with information overload. The media knows this and relies on the cognitive bias to manipulate you into believing things that are simply not true. Things that lead to cognitive bias maybe just reading the headline and not the full story. Headlines can be misleading and are also used as clickbait. It's usually a controversial headline that sparks your curiosity, but when you click on it, there is little content. The source makes money on the number of clicks they receive. Other things that can lead to cognitive bias are who wrote the piece or who in your social network has shared it. If these are people that you know, like or trust, you are more apt to believe the story. The media knows this and sends you the information you are most likely to believe.

Journalists are supposed to be fair and unbiased. Now we have reporters that wear a particular team's jersey on the air. We used to call them homers, and that was not a compliment. Unbiased journalism is reporting the facts and allowing the audience to make up their own minds about the story. When journalists associate themselves with the success of a team, they can use their platform to plant stories. Stories that can get people hired or fired. I have had conversations with fans that are telling me things about the team that I know for a fact are not true, yet I can't convince them that it is fake news. The NBA draft can be manipulated by the media, and management has to make the decision that is best for the team, not the most popular one. Kristaps Porzingis was a no brainer as the fourth pick in the 2015 draft, yet the New York Knicks fans booed when Phil Jackson picked him. The media were pushing the Knicks away from Porzingis, and the fans were manipulated into believing he was the wrong pick. History has proven Phil made the right choice.

More than ever, I see so-called journalists allying themselves with certain people, whether it's a coach, executive, owner, or agent. They act as mouthpieces for these people, writing stories that flatter them and protect them in exchange for access. They spin a tale so well it's as if they are acting as a PR director for the team or individual.

Some of the fake news is downright comical like Kobe coming out of retirement to play outfield for the Los Angeles Dodgers, but most of it is egregious. Maybe the most shocking use of fake news is agents planting stories about players and coaches. I know for a fact that agents have put out misleading information to orchestrate trades or get coaches hired or fired.

They have even propagated bogus health information in an attempt to cover the ineptitude of a player. I was confronted by an agent in public at a restaurant on the road. His client had been playing poorly coming off an injury. This is not uncommon for many players when returning to play. Returning to play is more than just being healthy enough to play. There is timing and conditioning. No matter what we do in practice, we cannot reproduce the speed and power of a real game. No matter how much you scrimmage, it's not the same. The last piece of the puzzle in return to play is actually to play. Most times, the team and fans are understanding and patient of the process. This agent could not understand why I wouldn't make up an injury for him to cover for his client's poor performance. He didn't last long with the Lakers and has bounced from team to team tweeting the same excuses expecting people to believe them.

It's become the big joke: "I saw it on the internet, so it must be true."

I learned how to spot fake news by:

1. Consider the source of the information

2. Read beyond the headline but don't fall for clickbait

3. Be aware of your own cognitive bias

CHAPTER 21

THE OFFICIALS

As a child, my parents told me to never talk to strangers, but if I were lost, I could always trust a police officer or fireman. We were raised to have respect for people in uniform, whether they were cops, firemen, or armed forces. This rang true for me since these were occupations that I had no interest in. It takes a particular personality to put themselves in the center of violence or turmoil. I'll fight if I have to, but I'm not the kind of guy that goes looking to break up fights. I want to think I would go into a burning building to save my loved ones, but I don't want to make a living saving people from burning buildings.

On May 8th, 1972, President Richard Nixon agreed to a cease-fire in Vietnam, and by January 1973 a peace treaty was signed. I was 18 years old in 1972, which was draft age. If the war continued I most likely would have gone to Vietnam, but there's no way I would have volunteered for it. I was walking down the hall of my dorm freshman year in college when I got the news I wasn't going to war. It was one of the most memorable days of my life. As a result, I have always had a soft spot in my heart for those who serve because I didn't want to. I've always been intrigued and respected those that voluntarily go into harm's way to save others.

Being an NBA official is not the same as being a cop, fireman, or soldier, but it is a position that comes with turmoil and sometimes violence. You may be on the court with other officials, but you're not really on a team. You may even have an official overrule your call which could be quite embarrassing. You have no fans, and you may call a maximum of 82 games, but none of them are home games. No one roots for the official. Both teams think they are getting screwed and think you are the one screwing them. They are supposed to be in charge but also invisible. The better they do their job, the more invisible they are. Personally, I think it's a thankless job and wondered why anyone would want to do it. Officials

196

get a bad rap, and I've always had a soft spot in my heart for them. I always tried to be the one kind face when they looked to the bench.

The game has changed drastically during my career, and officiating has changed with it. I came into the league when there were two officials per game for a total of 26 officials in the league. In 1988 a third official was put on the floor requiring the league to add 18 new officials to their roster. By the time I retired in 2016, there were 64 full-time NBA officials.

Hate is often rooted in ignorance, and that goes for those that hate NBA officials. They are human beings that are not infallible but are expected to be. They are required to process 97 possessions per team, which translates into 1000 decisions per game, and they do it with 92% accuracy. The coaches and players that are critical of them do not operate at 92% accuracy themselves but are quick to criticize the officiating. My only criticism of an official has been, does he or she hustle and were they in position to make the call.

When I watch a game, I'm trained to look at movement efficiency as well as body language and performance. In an attempt to make a case for NBA officials, I will give you my understanding of how they see the game. The triangle of NBA officiating begins with the lead official who is usually the most senior of the three. The lead official patrols the baseline, which is the best sightline of the whole court. The second most senior official is the trail and will be on the same side of the court as the ball (strong side). The lead official and the trail official being on the strong side is referred to as tandem officiating. The official with the least experience is in the slot. The slot is at the free throw line extended to the side line on the opposite side of the ball (weak side).

When I put it this way, it doesn't seem that complicated. Everyone has their spot to cover, but as the ball begins to move,

these positions become interchangeable. It wasn't as complicated in a half-court offensive set back in the '80s. With the
increased speed of a transition game, the official is put into a
position that is inconceivable to see all of the possible situations that could be against the rules. Add that to the fact that
you are officiating the most highly trained basketball players
in the world. They are not only looking for ways to take advantage of their opponent; they are looking at ways to take
advantage of the officials. An NBA official can make a pretty
good living, but it's not nearly close to the paychecks of the
other two entities on the floor. These are approximate salary
ranges for NBA players, coaches, and officials.

player $ 582,180 - $ 38,000,000

coach $ 2,500,000 - $ 11,000,000

official $150,000 - $ 550,000

You are required to be physically trained. The league has
camera technology and algorithms to determine the load on
each player during the course of a game. If a player plays 48
minutes, it's front-page news. All three NBA officials are working every minute of a 48-minute game plus overtime. They
must know the rules of the game and make split second decisions in front of millions of people. The rules are much more
complicated than you think.

There's even a case book that describes particular situations
that could come up in a game and how the rules should be
interpreted. There were many times controversial things happened in games in which the coach would tell me to go find
out. I would go to the case book only to learn the official was
right. These were seasoned and experienced coaches that
found out they were wrong, and the official got it right. It's not
easy to be an official, and the world does not understand that.
You can make an argument that these individuals could not

make that kind of money doing anything else. That may or may not be true. On one end of the spectrum, Bob Delaney was a veteran official that came from law enforcement. He was a New Jersey state trooper that went undercover into the mob. Law enforcement certainly seems like a natural transition to a higher paying rule enforcement job. The other end of the spectrum was long-time official Dick Bavetta. He was a stockbroker before he went into officiating full time. I'm sure he was making a good living working at the exchange. I don't think money has anything to do with it. I think there are people out there that believe in the rules and they have a certain self-satisfaction in being the one to enforce them. They have a union and lobby for more money, but it's not about the money.

There has been a lot written about the psychology of following the rules. The bottom line is there has to be respect for the rules which comes from fear of the consequences if they are not followed. I asked many officials during my career; why do you want to be an official? The simple answer is always for the love of the game. I believe that but I also believe that it is psychologically deeper than that. The best of the game comes out when it's played fairly and both teams can compete on a level playing field. It is the official's job to make that happen. It's more than just the love of the game for them. It's having so much respect for the game that they want it to be played the right way, and they are willing to put themselves on the firing line for that opportunity.

I often cringed when I heard the way certain coaches and players berated officials. It sets a bad example for the fans. A coach publicly humiliating an official can create an open season on him or her from the crowd. The game then becomes about the officials and not the players. The children attending the games may learn that this behavior is ok if the parent does not take the time to explain what is acceptable and what is not on the playing field. It's ok to question a call. It's not ok to attack an official verbally or physically for a bad call. When we allow this behavior to go on in front of our children, they become conditioned to repeat what they saw in the big leagues. Parents that don't teach their children that disrespecting an official may see the same behavior played out in their youth leagues. Parents attacking officials in front of young kids happens all of the time, and professional sports has done nothing to condemn this behavior other than issuing fines. Professional sports across the board has been negligent in educating the public about officiating.

Maybe if fans knew more about the whys and hows to becoming an official, there would be greater respect for them and more tolerance in our society. We often talk about how much our youth can learn by participating in sports. Up until now, we have completely missed this opportunity of using officials to teach our youth conflict resolution.

CHAPTER 22

THE LETTER

November 7, 1991, Magic Johnson retired after learning he tested positive for HIV. Even though he retired, the fans voted him to the NBA All-Star team with the second most votes behind Clyde Drexler. This magnanimous jesture came with tremendous controversy throughout the league. At the time, HIV was thought to be a highly contagious disease contracted and transmitted by gay individuals and IV drug users. Since it was presumed Magic was not an IV drug user, he must be gay. This assumption was also fueled by a rumor started by one of Magic's former friends that was still in the league.

None the less despite the undercurrent of some players, coaches and league execs opposing his participation in the game, Magic called David Stern and asked if he could play. Magic was haunted by the fact that he wasn't able to go out on his own terms and this was his chance to begin a comeback. He later said if he knew then what he knew now about HIV, he never would have retired. I agree with that logic, but he still would have had to go public to inform the many women he had sexual relations with so they could be screened.

It would have been a great way to educate the world that HIV positive people are not to be feared, but we would have been in the same learning curve. The debate over his ability to play was sparked immediately upon his announcement, and you must commend David Stern on his actions. He instinctively set out to educate himself and the league about HIV. He sent experts to every team to quell the fears from the owners down to the ball boys.

Despite his best efforts to educate and suppress the fears, there was still a group of individuals that were quite vocal about their opposition to being forced to play with a known HIV positive player. Stern had a lot on his plate. If he did not allow Magic to play, there could have been discrimination lawsuits. There were sponsorship considerations. Were there other HIV positive players that would lead to league-wide mandatory screening? Would HIV screening be a violation of the player's civil rights.? Stern showed tremendous leadership at a critical time that had repercussions around the world. He used NBA basketball to change the perception of HIV.

Magic went on to play in the All-Star game scoring 25 points on 9 for 12 shooting. He also had nine assists, was voted MVP and finished the game with an iconic 3 point shot. Stern hugged Magic at half court, and the controversy was diffused, or so we thought.

Playing in the All-Star game was the first step of Magic's comeback. Next, he decided to keep his spot on the Olympic team dubbed the Dream Team. This not only reignited the controversy, it now became global. An Australian official recommended boycotting the games, and one of their players said he would rather take silver than play against Magic which made me laugh. Whether Magic played or not, it was still a dream team, and the best Australia was going to do was silver. They ended up not medaling at all. The Dream Team won gold, Croatia won silver and Lithuania won bronze. Magic Johnson co-captained the Dream Team with Larry Bird. They outscored their opponents by an average of 43 points per game and Magic showed the world he could still play with HIV.

The next order of business was his return to the NBA.

Back in the '80s and 90's the NBA preseason games were put on by promoters. They would match two teams, rent an arena, and guarantee each side a certain amount of money to play.

There was usually some hook to the marketing like two former college teammates now in the NBA playing on different teams competing against each other at their alma mater. The 1992 matchup between the Los Angeles Lakers and the Cleveland Cavaliers was played at the University of North Carolina Dean

Dome and featured James Worthy vs. Brad Daugherty. They were not teammates, but they were both coached by Dean Smith at UNC, and Tar Heel fans would come out to see them play. At the time the Lakers and Cavs agreed to play we did not know Magic Johnson would come out of retirement. The controversy continued with players becoming very vocal about their fears playing with Magic.

The two most notable were Karl Malone of the Utah Jazz and Mark Price who was the point guard for the Cavaliers, the team we were about to play. Before Magic's comeback, I went through an HIV education, mostly with our team physician, Dr. Mickey Mellman. My knowledge about HIV went from nil to much more than most. We even discussed that if there was blood on any player, I could hand them a gauze pad to apply to themselves to control the bleeding while I put the gloves on. I was asked by the NBA to write the protocol for blood-borne pathogens, and I created a video for Healthsouth physical therapy clinics.

Because of Magic's compromised immune system, my focus was much more about protecting him from infection than the infinitesimal chance of him infecting someone else. I became a bit OCD about it. If we had a player on the team with the sniffles, I would tell Magic to stay away from him. This was new territory, and I was learning on the fly. Fatigue is a significant factor in the NBA and not a good thing for someone with HIV, so we decided to begin the preseason playing Magic every other game. We were 3 - 0 with him in the line up when we arrived in Chapel Hill to play our eighth and final preseason game on October 30, 1992, a date that will haunt me the rest of my life.

Magic was fouled driving to the basket, and one of our players Sean Rooks, alerted me that Magic had an open wound on his forearm. As he was going to the line to shoot the free throws, I told official Eddie Rush to check it out. Neither he nor Magic could see the cut, that's how insignificant it was. The next time out, I got nosey and checked it out for myself. It was a small fingernail scratch that was a non-bloody wound in a controlled situation, but now everyone was aware of it. All eyes were upon me, our players, coaches, fans, and cameras.

Once again, my focus was on covering it to protect Magic from everyone else. I knew he was a threat to no one. My training with Dr. Mellman kicked in. I sprayed a 6-inch cotton tip applicator with tough skin to make the skin around the scratch stickie then applied a band-aid without ever touching the wound. I had gloves in my back pocket and considered putting them on as per the protocol. What Magic didn't know, was while Karl Malone and other players were complaining publicly, his own teammates were coming to me privately asking; "I have to practice with this guy are you sure this is ok." How could I tell them, yes it's ok, and then he sustains a fingernail scratch that is a non-bloody wound, and I don gloves? It was a mixed message that I was unwilling to send. Magic saw the same fear on everyone's face that I saw. In this one moment playing basketball was no longer fun for Magic and he decided to retire for a second time.

When he announced the retirement, he was on the front page of every newspaper in the world, but he wasn't alone. I was dead center in the picture with my 6-inch cotton tip applicator and no gloves. Things went from bad to worse. An anonymous Rhode Island doctor filed a formal complaint against me with the Occupational Safety and Health Administration (OSHA). To this day, I don't know who or why. It was intimated to me by one of the investigators that it might have been an overzealous Celtics fan. There were some people that weren't happy with me for not gloving, namely David Stern and Jerry West. It crushed me that I disappointed Jerry West, but I stood by my actions and explained why I did what I did in the hopes I wouldn't get fired. The investigation took a year. When the door is open for OSHA to come in, they come in for everything. The genesis of the investigation was about me and the gloves, but it went far beyond that to how the Forum was run. Things like were there signs to instruct operations staff to bend their knees when lifting to hand washing instructions. In the end, I was exonerated by OSHA, but it was page eight news. I was a hero to many in the gay and HIV community but also received a couple of scathing letters from xenophobes.

Once it finally blew over, I was able to return to the good graces of David Stern and Jerry West, but it was almost 25 years later that I received the formal vindication that would become the prize possession of my career. After my retirement, I received a letter from NBA Commissioner Adam Silver. It reads:

Dear Gary,

I write to thank you for 32 years of outstanding service to the Los Angeles Lakers and the NBA. As a fixture on our sidelines and as one of the top athletic trainers in the world, you played a critical role in the eight Lakers championships, keeping your players healthy and strong. Your support of Magic Johnson through his HIV diagnosis - as a friend and as a trainer - will never be forgotten. It helped diminish the stigma associated with the virus and encouraged others around the world to treat those infected with HIV and AIDS with dignity and respect.

Throughout your career, you've also demonstrated a remarkable commitment to sharing your knowledge with other coaches, trainers, and doctors, and as a result, players throughout the league have benefitted from your unparalleled experience.

Thank you again for all you've done for the Lakers, the NBA and the game of basketball. It's been a pleasure working with you, and I wish you all the best in the future.

Warm regards,
Adam

NATIONAL BASKETBALL ASSOCIATION

ADAM SILVER
COMMISSIONER

April 1, 2016

Mr. Gary Vitti
636 13th Street
Manhattan Beach, CA 90266

Dear Gary,

I write to thank you for 32 years of outstanding service to the Los Angeles Lakers and the NBA. As a fixture on our sidelines and as one of the top athletic trainers in the world, you played a critical role in eight Lakers championships, keeping your players healthy and strong. Your support of Magic Johnson through his HIV diagnosis – as a friend and as a trainer – will never be forgotten. It helped diminish the stigma associated with the virus and encouraged others around the world to treat those infected with HIV and AIDS with dignity and respect.

Throughout your career you've also demonstrated a remarkable commitment to sharing your knowledge with other coaches, trainers and doctors, and as a result, players throughout the league have benefited from your unparalleled experience.

Thank you again for all you've done for the Lakers, the NBA and the game of basketball. It's been a pleasure working with you, and I wish you all the best in the future.

Warm regards,

Adam

Olympic Tower, 645 Fifth Avenue, New York, NY 10022 • asilver@nba.com • 212-407-8060

I don't know if Adam actually wrote it or if one of his people did, but he signed it, and even if he didn't write it, someone did and recognized my actions in regards to the Magic Johnson/HIV nightmare. Till this day Magic and I have never discussed that fateful moment in Chapel Hill. He never brought it up, nor did I but of all my rings and memorabilia it's that letter that I'm most proud of which has become my most prized career possession.

CHAPTER 23

THE IMPORTANCE OF A MENTOR

I want to tell you a story about a great man. His name is Bill Sharman. When I was growing up back east as a New York Knicks fan in the '70s, there were only 17 teams in the NBA. I remember listening to games on the radio called by the famous Marty Glickman and later on WOR-TV by the voice of the Knicks Marv Albert. I never had the opportunity to meet Marty, but I met Marv many times, and there is no better announcer nor better guy to be around than Marv Albert. There were many times I had to pinch myself when he would be doing a national broadcast of a Lakers game, and we would spend some time together knowing this was the guy I was listening to as a kid and now I'm talking to him, and he knows who I am.

There was no ESPN, TNT, etc. like there is today, and it seemed like the only games I was able to tune in were the Knicks vs. the Celtics or the Philadelphia 76ers. As a result, I knew of three coaches, all of whom I was able to meet during my time with the Lakers. Tommy Heinsohn was the coach of the Celtics, Jack Ramsay with the 76ers and my hero Red Holzman coached the Knicks.

Tommy and I met many times in the '80s and even though he was a Celtic and I was a Laker I can honestly say he was pretty good to me and he didn't have to be. Jack Ramsey and I had a special relationship. He was the head coach of the Portland Trailblazers when I was at the University of Portland. Portland is sort of a small sports town and we were both there at the same time, so he knew I existed. He had a Doctorate in education and a keen interest in exercise physiology. He was a brilliant coach, and I always seemed to walk away from our conversations cerebrally stimulated.

But Red Holzman was my hero. He led the Knicks to two championships in 1970 and 1973. I had the fortunate experience to work with him at the 1997 NBA all-star game. It was the 50th anniversary of the NBA, and the league decided to honor the top 50 of all time. If there was ever an all-star game you wanted to work, this was the one. Before 1994 part of the weekend was the NBA Legends game that featured retired players from the eastern and western conference. The old-timers were sustaining serious injuries, and the legends game was replaced by the Rising Star Challenge which featured first and second-year players selected by assistant coaches.

The 1997 Rising Star Challenge game featured three Lakers, Kobe Bryant, Derek Fisher, and Travis Knight. The head coach for the eastern conference team was Red Auerbach, and the head coach for the west was Red Holzman. The athletic trainer for the east was my best friend in the league Gary Briggs and for the West was yours truly. Of all of the blessings I've had through my career, one of the highlights was working side by side with my hero Red Holzman.

He was truly a gentleman and relied heavily on me to make sure he was where he was supposed to be and when he was supposed to be there. Phil Jackson was coached by Red Holzman, and I once asked him what Red was like when he won or lost. Phil told me he would say after a win, I'm going home to Selma's (his wife) pot roast and a glass of scotch, and after a loss, I'm going home to Selma's pot roast and a glass of scotch. I appreciated that about Phil as well. He never got too high after a win or too low after a loss. I assume he inherited that trait from Red.

Growing up back east, I knew Bill Sharman played for the Celtics but who would have thought he would have such a great effect on my life. Bill was born in 1926 in Abilene, Texas. He graduated from the University of Southern California and played both professional baseball and basketball. His baseball career was with the Brooklyn Dodgers, and he played basketball for none other than the Boston Celtics from 1951 to 61. During his tenure as a star point guard, they won four championships. Following his retirement, Bill went into coaching and became the head coach of the Los Angeles Lakers in 1971. Before Bill's arrival, the Lakers lost to the Celtics 6 times in 8 years. During the 1971/72 championship season, he coached the Lakers to a 69 and 13 record. A record that lasted for 25 years. They also went on a 33 game winning streak that still stands today as an NBA record. Bill has been inducted into the Naismith Memorial Basketball Hall of Fame both as a player and a coach, one of only three people to hold that distinction.

He suffered a vocal cord injury after the 71/72 season which caused him to lose his voice and end his coaching career. But although he had great difficulty communicating without a voice, it never stopped him, and he found other ways to contribute by becoming the Lakers general manager, president, and later consultant. Ironically the Lakers had to hire their greatest nemesis, an ex Celtic to win a championship.

I learned from the history of the Lakers hiring Bill Sharman the importance of having a mentor. Mentoring helps people grow and stay on course. Until this day Bill's fingerprints are all over the legacy of the Los Angeles Lakers. The legacy and long term success of the franchise started with our mentor Bill Sharman and still lives on today. On the following page is one of the many notes that Bill Sharman gave me.

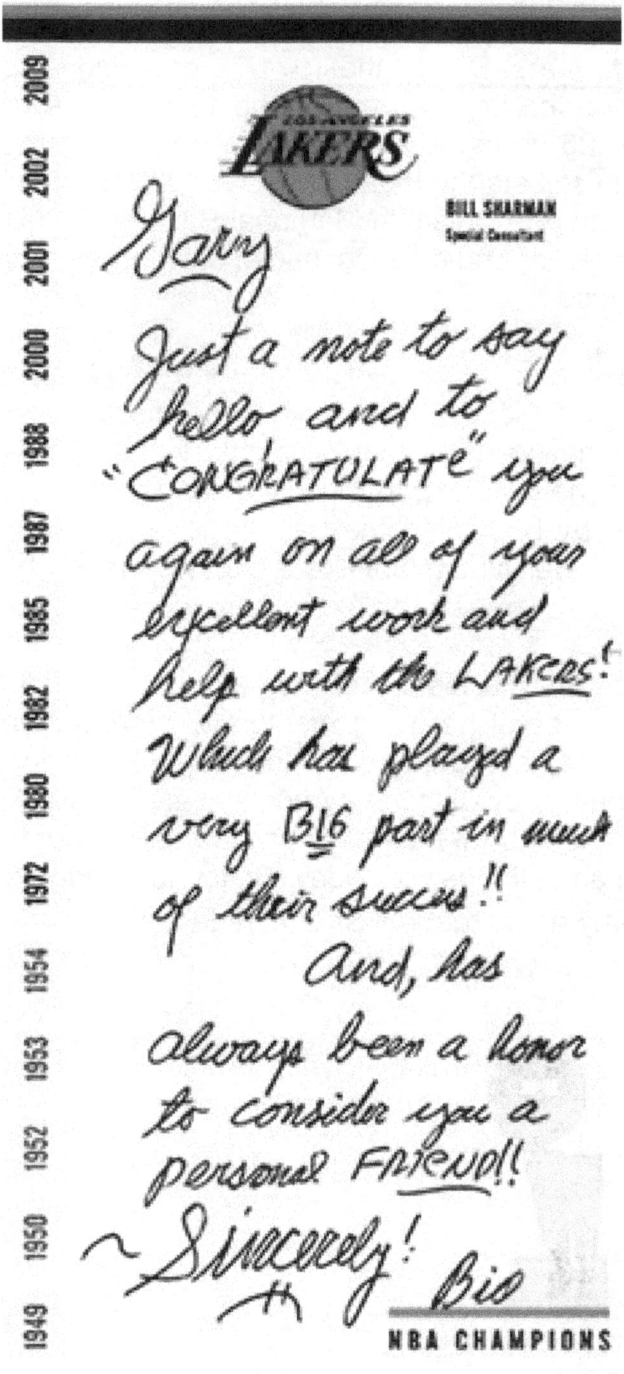

LOS ANGELES LAKERS

BILL SHARMAN
Special Consultant

2009 2002 2001 2000 1988 1987 1985 1982 1980 1972 1954 1953 1952 1950 1949

Gary

Just a note to say hello and to "CONGRATULATE" you again on all of your excellent work and help with the LAKERS! Which has played a very BIG part in much of their success!!

And, has always been a honor to consider you a personal FRIEND!!

~Sincerely!

Bill

NBA CHAMPIONS

CHAPTER 24

THE EVOLUTION OF SPORTS SCIENCE

Timing is one of the most important things in life, and the arc of my career is reflected in the timing of my life coinciding with the timing of the sports science revolution. I've always tried to pay attention to what the research showed and root my decisions on evidence-based practices. This wasn't always the easiest thing to do in a pro sports world where many players had their own gurus, quacks, snake oil salesmen, and pseudo-health-care professionals whispering in their ear.

Although there have been athletic trainers around since the gladiators, the field of sports medicine is very young. When I broke in, there were very few PH. D's in athletic training. I literally would have been one of the first. But now an athletic trainer with a PH. D, or ED. D after their name is the industry norm – especially since the advent of online degrees. When I graduated with a Master's degree in 1982, it was the beginning of a new wave of educated, athletic trainers that relied on evidence-based practices, not the old-style "I don't know why we do this, but it works" approach. And the field just keeps getting more and more sophisticated. There are thousands of younger, more educated athletic trainers graduating every year and using technology to reinforce what an athletic trainer does and why they do it.

There has been more progress made in understanding sports science and how best to achieve peak performance during the last ten years than in the previous 600 – or even 6,000 years. In historian David Webster's book, "The Iron Game: An Illustrated History of Weight Lifting." He goes all the way back to 3600 BC when Chinese emperors ordered their subjects to exercise to achieve better health that would make them more productive citizens.

My initial exposure to the first-wave fitness craze in the United States began with the President's Council on Physical Fitness. It was established by President Dwight D. Eisenhower in 1956, two years after I was born. The President's Council was created because of a series of articles published by Drs. Hans Kraus and Bonnie Prudden, who studied the fitness levels of America's youth and compared them to children from Switzerland, Italy, and Austria. The results were shocking to a country that had just saved the World from Hitler's tyranny and justifiably considered itself exceptional: the post World War II youth of America failed miserably compared to their European counterparts. Our mid-century post-war prosperity was making our kids soft and self-satisfied.

So, the "fitness gap" alarm was sounded. Suddenly the kids in local schools were doing jumping jacks, playing kickball and dodge ball in gym class and running around the track with teachers holding stop-watches to monitor their times.

By 1961, when I was seven years old, President John F. Kennedy, acting on his pledge to get America moving again, launched an even more aggressive physical fitness campaign by speaking at conferences and releasing educational films. It was the beginning of a movement that has lasted far longer than anyone could have imagined back then.

Thanks to those long-ago efforts by Eisenhower and Kennedy, the baby boomers born between 1946 and 1964 -- the second largest segment of our population behind millennials -- as well as the generations that followed us are more active than our parents, who got most of their exercise from doing their jobs and tending to their homes and gardens. The Boomers are interested in not only living a long life but also in having a healthy, active quality of life in their golden years. But I worry that the millennials spend too much time with their phones and video screens and don't get enough exercise. The modern fitness movement took a huge step forward in 1968 when Dr. Ken Cooper wrote the book "Aerobics." It not only introduced a new term into the pop vocabulary, but it put the focus squarely on developing cardiopulmonary (heart and lung) ca-

215

pacity in addition to building up your muscles. An off-shoot of the new emphasis on aerobics was the explosion in jogging, as millions of sedentary types got off the couch and became addicted to their aerobic high of pleasurable endorphins released in the brain.

Cooper was an Air Force doctor who studied military personnel and originated the concept that aerobic exercise could preserve your health. He defined aerobic exercise as low to medium intensity workouts over extended periods of time that used oxygen to obtain energy from both fat and glycogen, which is energy stored in your muscles.

He became widely known as the "Father of Aerobics" and established the Cooper Institute in Dallas, Texas to continue studying this concept. His research and recommendations helped millions of people live long, active, healthy lives. He is a seminal figure in the evolution of modern physical fitness concepts and ideas.

Indeed, Cooper's work was a big influence on my training philosophy for the Lakers. At our mandatory pre-season physical exams, I had all of our players stress-tested for cardiac anomalies before the intensive workouts began. But I also had them tested for VO2 max – their lung capacity -- to determine their fitness levels coming into training camp. The top two performers were AC Green and Michael Cooper, and I was third.

Beyond that, I also initiated the 20/20 rule. If a player did not play at least 20 minutes in a game, then he owed me a 20-minute aerobic workout after the game. It could be on a treadmill or a stationary bike or even just jogging around the court for at least 20 minutes. I set that as the minimum time because the data at that time showed that this was the threshold of the benefits of an aerobic workout.

Many times, especially early on, I had several bench players ask me what this had to do with playing basketball. I had to patiently explain that being aerobically fit had everything to do with being able to play basketball effectively and efficiently for more than five minutes at a time.

The American College of Sports Medicine (ACSM) said that aerobic exercise needed to be done at least three times per week for at least 20 minutes per session to be fully effective. As an athletic trainer that made his reputation by staying close to the evidence-based research published in double-blind peer-reviewed journals, I could explain to the players -- and management -- that this 20-minute rule was vital to keeping our players in the best possible condition. And I had the ACSM and the Cooper Clinic to back me up.

The next big step forward for training NBA players was introducing them to strength training. At the time I became the Lakers head athletic trainer in the summer of 1984 strength training – anaerobic exercise -- was almost non-existent. At the same time, more studies were coming out that proved basketball was not exclusively an aerobic exercise, as was the common belief at the time. Instead, research showed that it combined elements of both aerobic and anaerobic exercise, categorizing the sport as being on the aerobic/anaerobic threshold. Thus, I changed our post-game drills from continuous running to mixing up running with interval training.

Anaerobic exercise is a high-intensity activity that lasts for short periods of time. It is an exercise that is not dependent on oxygen to deliver energy to your muscles. Strength training, or resistance training, as it is sometimes called, has been around for a long time – the ancient Greeks lifted stones for exercise -- and was typically the exercise of choice for most physical fitness buffs prior to Dr. Cooper introducing aerobics in the late '60s.

Strength training fell into two categories: the first was called powerlifting which back in the '60s was best exemplified by Russian strong-man Vasily Alekseyev, a bulked-up beast who was built like a cross between a refrigerator and a fire hydrant. He was famous as the World's Strongest Man because he could lift up to 560 pounds at a time.

The other category was called Body Building, favored by guys like Arnold Schwarzenegger and Lou Ferrigno, who concentrated on building up specific muscle groups and making sure their body was lean, symmetrical and looked good. It had been around since the late 1930s in gyms like Vic Tanny's or the YMCA. There was even a well-known advertising campaign for Charles Atlas workouts in the 1950s in which a 90-pound weakling at the beach had sand kicked in his face by a buff-built bully who always got the girl. In the ads, the puny guy started bodybuilding and got big enough to fight back – and in the process, steal the girl from the bully. You knew it was true because there was a picture of the new bodybuilder in a Speedo suit holding the bikini-clad girl in his suddenly-enlarged arms.

In 1965 Joe Gold opened the first Gold's Gym in Venice Beach, which quickly became synonymous with Muscle Beach, the out-door workout area near the gym. Joe was a guy with a macho attitude that matched his muscles.

I met Gold early in my NBA career when most teams did not have their own training facilities. Strength training was still controversial. Most players were reluctant to lift weights because they felt they would become muscle-bound and lose their shooting touch and their feel for the game.

The Lakers practiced at Loyola Marymount University, which had a rich basketball tradition but a weak weight room because they didn't have a football program. So, I started looking elsewhere for a venue to conduct our strength training. By the time I met Joe Gold, he had built World's Gym in Venice

Beach. Arnold and other well-known bodybuilders like Lou Ferrigno were always working out at Worlds. After just one visit I quickly realized this was the spot I was looking for and Joe eagerly welcomed the Lakers. It was good for the Lakers, good for Joe's business, and even good for myself when I ended up training with Ferrigno for a whole year in preparation for his last Masters Mr. Olympia competition. He finished second, and the workouts which I participated in became part of the footage for his autobiographical film Standing Tall.

World's gym was an atmosphere of heavy iron. It was nothing like today's plush health clubs or even a YMCA-like environment. No juice bar, massage room, or jacuzzi. This was a hard-nosed, hard-working gym. If you were soft, you took plenty of heat from the men and women who came there to work out. There was a reputation to live up to if you entered the gym. If you didn't fit in or measure up, you were laughed at and taunted for your lack of work ethic. I remember one regular saying to underachievers, "are you a barbarian or a librarian?" And there was no doubt which one he preferred. The intensity level was perfect for a group of professional basketball players, many of whom had never before been in the weight room or been around that type of workout intensity.

World's gym achieved such notoriety – thanks at least in part to the documentary "Pumping Iron" – that for people traveling to Southern California it became a dream destination where they could work out, buy a T-shirt and go home to prove they were there. Kind of like Disneyland or the Universal Studio Tour, but with a lot more sweat and without the glitz and glamour.

For all of our training methods, I always asked myself three basic questions: What am I trying to do? Why am I doing it? And how will I do it? My approach in introducing players to strength training was no different. At that time the Showtime Lakers were a running team, a team of sleek thoroughbreds like Magic Johnson, James Worthy, Byron Scott, and Michael Cooper. So my goal was not to make them better athletes -- they were already the best in the world!

My goal was to prepare them to do battle against Eastern Conference teams like the Boston Celtics, Detroit Pistons and Philadelphia 76ers. These teams were very physical and played a style we called goon ball – which meant allowing no lay-ups, a lot of holding, arm locking and an understanding that if you were going to be called for a foul it might as well be a hard foul that drove your opponent to the floor and made him think twice about coming into the lane, which was the big man's territory. Back then hand-checking your man was also allowed, which gave the goon teams yet another advantage.

Coach Pat Riley and I both knew we had to bulk up to match their lunch-pail, hard-hat mentality. So my goal at World's Gym was to make our players stronger to be able to withstand the physical confrontations in the painted area under the basket and strong enough to reduce injury risk. There was little if anything in the literature other than reps and sets to give me guidance but the bodybuilding paradigm made sense to me: gain lean mass and be symmetric – making sure the right side of the body looks like the left side. Reps and sets were based on the work of the Hungarian endocrinologist Hans Selye's model called the General Adaptation Syndrome, from his research in the 1950s. His concept of dividing training into phases was later expanded on by Russian physiologist Leo Matveyev, who studied the training programs and successes of the 1952 and 1956 summer Olympic athletes. His research was used to create the famous "periodization model" for the Russians to compete in the 1960 Olympics.

The model was then spread throughout the eastern European bloc by Matveyev and Romanian born Tudor Bompa, who I had the pleasure of meeting and lecturing with at a conference in Shanghai, China in 2016. With the fall of the Soviet

Union in 1989, the work of Sele, Matveyev, and Bompa was picked up first in Germany and then the rest of the world. This model became my bible. Although it has been modified and become more evidence-based for the modern-day athlete, it is still the foundation of all training today.

In his regular life, Joe Gold was a machinist, and he thought there was another way of resistance training besides moving barbells, plates, and dumbbells around. They were large metal frames that had airplane cables that went around pulleys that were attached to stacks of rectangular weighted plates. It was perfect for some of our players that had difficulty controlling lifts because of the length of their arms and legs.

Weight lifting can be quite addictive to many people, so keeping our strength training in perspective was important. We were not there to become bodybuilders or powerlifters. We were there to help us become better basketball players. I designed the programs with the basics like working for larger muscle groups first then smaller groups later and paying close attention to push exercises like bench presses vs. pull exercises as lat pulls. I soon learned that for every push exercise, we needed three pull exercises to maintain musculoskeletal balance. Joe Gold making machines for strength training was a step forward in terms of targeting specific muscle groups.

Then around 1970, Arthur Jones created the Nautilus system. Jones' big idea was to move away from the kind of training Joe Gold and Arnold advocated of using free weights for hours at a time. He designed a program of high-intensity training involving short, single sets, done with maximum intensity, to maximize muscular growth.

It was the advent of Nautilus machines that made resistance training appealing to the general public, fueling the fitness boom of the 1970s and 80's and resulting in Nautilus gyms in strip malls across America. Looking at the musculoskeletal

221

system as a group of levers and fulcrums, it's simple physics to see that we are at mechanical advantages through certain parts of our range of motion when lifting a weight.

For example: when a sprinter gets down into the blocks to start a race, the blocks are not set at random. They are set so that when the gun goes off the sprinter is in the best mechanical position to give them the most power at the moment of takeoff. Similarly, when you do a curl, it's harder to initiate the exercise when your elbow is straight. As you get past the initial range of motion, the exercise is easier, and at the end of the range when your elbows are completely bent, the exercise is effortless.

This is because of mechanical advantages throughout your range of motion. If you were to work your muscles maximally in the middle of the range, you would be unable to get the exercise started from the straight elbow position. This is why Arthur Jones created the nautilus system that varied the resistance throughout the range of motion by running the cable around a kidney-shaped cam as opposed to a pulley. The cam would vary the resistance as the cable went around the cam through the lift. State of the art technology, right? It's a good idea, but the problem was that James Worthy is 6' 9", and I'm 5' 9", and we're working on the same machine and the same cam with the only adjustment being to raise or lower the seat. It seemed like a pretty good idea at the time, but it didn't work.

The concept of variable resistance was born by Arthur Jones and Nautilus, but the geniuses at Lumenx corp figured out the only way to actually work a muscle maximally through the range of motion is to control the speed of the contraction. In 1974 we saw the concept of Isokinetics come to life with the Cybex machine.

Every training room either had a Cybex or wanted a Cybex to

test and/or train their athletes. The Cybex was a machine with a lever arm that would attach to an upper or lower limb. The other end of the lever arm was attached to a dynamometer with a preset speed that no matter how hard you pushed against the lever arm you couldn't make it go faster than the speed it was preset at through the full range of motion. As a result, you were getting a maximum contraction through the range. It then had a running tape in which a needle printed a strength curve measured in foot-pounds to tell the practitioner how much force was being generated and wherein the range it was being generated -- or more importantly not being generated. This could tell us where in the range of motion, the athletes had a strength deficit. It was state of the art technology, and I wanted to be part of it, so I did my master's thesis, "The effects of variable training speeds on leg strength and power" using a Cybex.

As they say, when you have a new hammer, everything looks like a nail. The electronically speed-controlled Cybex was expensive and better served for rehab and testing, so Lumenx came out with a training version called the Orthotron, which controlled the speed with hydraulic valves. It quickly appeared in weight rooms and training rooms across the country. The state of the art technology concept of Isokinetics all sounded pretty good until 1995 when Dr. Arthur Stiendler broke down the kinetic chain into open kinetic chain and closed kinetic chain exercises.

The Cybex isokinetic machine is an open chain, meaning non-weight bearing. Although the definition of closed chain exercises can be a bit nebulous, my definition of closed chain is: performing an exercise in a weight-bearing position with movement in more than one joint and more than one plane. This allows for exercises that are more functional to athletic movement and the activities of daily life.

As a result, the technology progressed to training athletes

with closed kinetic chain exercises. The Cybex machine soon became a comfy seat in the training room for an athlete that was waiting his turn to get on a treatment table.

Dr. Vladimir Janda is a Czechoslovakian neurologist who contracted polio. As a result of his affliction, he studied the human neuromuscular system. Beginning in 1983 he categorized individuals into three postural distortion patterns he called upper crossed syndrome, lower closed syndrome and pronation distortion syndrome. Prior to Janda, we looked at the muscular system as either being a primary or secondary mover for certain muscle action. Janda figured out that the musculoskeletal system was more complicated than just primary or secondary movers. There was also a stabilization muscle group.

The movement groups were prone to tightness and needed to be released and stretched while the stabilization groups were weak and needed to be activated. He was able to then identify if you had one of the three postural distortion syndromes and he would know which muscles to release and stretch and which to activate – which not only made you feel better but actually corrected your posture. The Janda method opened up the technology in the early '80s that allowed us to look at the body in a different way and also gave us an avenue for correction.

It was a breakthrough and a good start, but the issue was that it was an evaluation of static posture. Static posture is assessing posture while the athlete is standing in front of you in their normal stance without movement. We wanted to look at posture dynamically -- meaning one's posture as they are moving through space.

A dynamic postural evaluation allows us to make a better determination of your movement efficiency. We want to know how you are transferring force from your lower extremity through your pelvis to your upper body and/or transferring force from the upper body through your pelvis to your lower extremities. In 1995 Gray Cook created the Functional Movement Screen (FMS). He put you through 7 functional movement patterns: squatting, stepping, lunging, reaching, leg raising, push up, and rotary stability. You are graded on each functional movement from 0—3. The maximum score if you can do all of the movements with good function and pain-free is 21. Longitudinal research in the National Football League tells us players with scores below 14 are at greater risk of injury. Gray Cook went on to create a second platform called Selective Functional Movement Assessment (SFMA) for individuals who had an injury or pain with performing the FMS. The FMSA used 7 top tier movements: cervical movement, upper extremity movement, multi-segmental flexion, multi-segmental rotation, multi-segment extension, single-leg stance, and the squatting pattern. Although there has been skepticism regarding the validity and reliability of the FMS and SFMA platforms, they were excellent at the time.

As recently as 2013, Mike Clarke created the Fusionetics platform. Similar to the FMS and SFMA, Fusionetics was a functional movement screening platform. The functional movements in the Fusionetics platform are: double leg squat, double leg squat with a heel lift, single-leg squat, push up shoulder movement, trunk/lumbar spine movement, and cervical spine movement. After completing the assessment, there is a 0—100 score on movement efficiency. The platform uses a stoplight like a red, yellow, and green zone. Scores from 75—100 are in a green zone, and that athlete has good movement efficiency. Scores between 74.9 and 50 are in the yellow zone having moderate movement efficiency and a score between 49.99—0 has poor movement efficiency.

The Fusionetics platform has software that assesses your movement efficiency according to your score and gives you exact corrective exercises through a proprietary app on your cell phone or tablet. To date, in my humble opinion, Mike

Clarke and his Fusionetics platform has done more for evaluation and correction than any individual in the history of sports medicine.

With the exception of the latest Fusionetics platform, all these technologies rely on subjective analysis – what you see with the human eye. We have now entered an age of wireless technology that allows us to use high-speed cameras and sensors that shoot hundreds of times per second to give us objective information like: leg symmetry, ground reaction force, acceleration, deceleration, ground contact time, steps per minute, distance, speed, tibial inclination, valgus/varus movement (i.e., knock-kneed or bow-legged), range of motion, quality of movement, balance and more. We have taken the human error out of the physical assessment and created a platform to first objectively identify one's mechanical deficiencies, and then correct those deficiencies prior to entering their performance training and competition phase. We can also continue to monitor that training to know how much to push and maybe more importantly, how much is too much to reduce injury risk and maximize performance.

Man's desire to capture human motion can be traced back to 1878 with Eadweard Muybridges's desire to answer the question: are all four of horse's hooves off the ground during a trot. Muybridge created a system lined with still life cameras whose triggers were connected by a string. As the horse ran across a racetrack, the cameras would snap still shots in sequence to give a series of consecutive photos. He then created a device to rotate the photos in the order they were taken. Hence the first motion picture was born.

By the mid-1980s, I was introduced to rotoscoping, which used visible markers on an athlete to encode a three-dimensional stick figure that we used for biomechanical analysis to enhance performance and reduce injury. Today, we have high-speed camera technology and algorithms to create a three-dimensional kinematic model. Couple high-speed camera technology with high-speed wearable sensors and we have today's state of the art ability to analyze motion and measure the daily load on an athlete.

This state of the art technology allows the practitioner to objectively measure what the athlete is doing and how the athlete is responding to what is being done to him or her. This information is important for the first evaluation and correction and then return to play. Generally speaking, tissue healing time is 6 to 8 weeks, followed by the remodeling phase. The remodeling phase is the adaptation to the loads put upon that tissue. At six weeks, although the injured tissue has healed and matured, there still needs to be additional stimulation of new tissue to support the load of exercise. If the healed tissue is under-stimulated, it will be too weak to meet the demands of the load. If the healed tissue is overstimulated, it will go through a metabolic change. These metabolic changes could result in stress reactions and/or stress fractures for bone and tendinitis and/or tendinosis/tendinopathy for a tendon. There is a sweet spot that is the correct amount of stress to apply to healing tissues to ensure the athlete can meet specific exercise demands, and this is where today's technology can help the athlete return from practice to competition safely.

Technology needs to be valid, reliable, and practical. Validity studies insure the technology does what the manufacturer claims it does. Reliability means that it accurately and repeatedly does it. For instance, a technology may do what the manufacturer claims, but its accuracy is inconsistent. There are cases when a technology is valid and reliable, but it's impractical. I recently witnessed a sensor technology demo. The technology provided a significant amount of valid and reliable data, but the athlete had to wear a dozen or more sensors. This technology may be practical for a movement efficiency baseline and intermittent tests for bio-mechanics, but it wouldn't work for daily use, which is where most technologies exist today. After technology gives us an objective evaluation of the athlete's movement efficiency, it can also give us an objective measurement to manage workload. Load is a combination of physical stressors and non-physical stressors. The external stimulus applied to an individual is referred to as an external load, which can be measured by:

GPS
ACCELEROMETERS
GYROSCOPES
CHRONOMETERS
DYNAMOMETERS
CAMERA TECHNOLOGY

Internal load is the physiological and psychological response to external load combined with non-physical stressors. Gabbett's work reported in the British Journal of Sports Medicine states that Internal load is measured by a Rated Perception of Exertion (RPE) scale. The scale ranges from 0=rest to 10=max difficulty. Combining the RPE with the duration of a workout, we can monitor the response of the load on an athlete and then create an acute (7 days) to chronic (28 days) workload ratio.

SESSION LOAD = *RPE X DURATION (in Minutes)*
DAILY LOAD = *SUM OF ALL SESSION LOADS IN A 24 HOUR PERIOD*
WEEKLY LOAD = *SUM OF ALL DAILY LOADS FOR 7 DAYS*
MONOTONY = *ONE STANDARD DEVIATION OF WEEKLY LOAD*
STRAIN = *DAILY OR WEEKLY LOAD X MONOTONY*

Optimal monitoring of workload requires a daily monitoring of internal and external load and monitoring the acute to chronic workload ratio. Hulin et al. report in the British Journal of Sports Medicine that the higher the acute workload compared to the chronic workload, the greater fatigue factor, and the higher risk of injury. Technology helps us determine where the earlier mentioned sweet spot is because it exists in a place where the acute work load never exceeds the chronic work-load. Foster et al. reported in the Wisconsin Medical Journal that 89% of injuries and illnesses correlated to a spike in strain ten days prior to the incident. Gabbett also reported that load increases equal to or greater than 15% from the preceding week increases injury risk by 50%.

This type of technology did not exist in the '80s and if it did the Lakers would have stood a better chance of threepeating in 1989. The Lakers swept three playoff rounds going 11 − 0 to get to the finals. The Detroit Pistons were in a heated six-game Eastern Conference series with the Bulls to return to a much-anticipated finals rematch. The Pistons were a physically and mentally tough-minded team that took us to a seven-game finals the prior year. Pat Riley knew that to threepeat there was going to be a dog fight because of the Pistons no mercy attitude.

Four days off in the NBA is an eternity, especially during a playoff run. No matter what a coach does in practice, he can never reproduce the speed, power, and intensity of a real game. It's hard to get the edge and even harder to keep the edge. We finished off the Phoenix Suns in a four-game sweep on May 28th to win the Western Conference and were not able to play the first game of the championship round until June 6th, an eight-day layoff. Riley decided to have an intense NBA playoff-type boot camp in Santa Barbara complete with training camp type conditioning and scrimmages.

On June 5th our starting two-guard Byron Scott during a live box out drill landed awkwardly and ruptured his hamstring. Three days later, on June 8th during the second quarter of game two Magic Johnson also suffered a moderate hamstring strain which he was unable to play with. Within four days we lost our starting backcourt for the finals. After going

229

11 – 0 to get to the finals, we were wounded animals and swept by the Detroit Pistons. We will never know if a healthy Lakers team could have pulled off the threepeat in 1989, but for sure it would have been a more even series. Coach Riley did what he thought was right. In those days, the mentality was to break through the wall both mentally and physically. Current longitudinal research tells us that breaking through the wall may not be the best approach. Today's technology gives us an objective view of postural distortion patterns that are difficult to see with even a trained naked eye. Through myofascial release and stretching of tight muscles and activation of weak muscles, we can get athletes out of their postural distortion patterns. These patterns have been developed from previous injury, repetitive movement, poor training habit, or a congenital anomaly.

The problem begins when the athlete fatigues and goes back into their default posture. This leads to poor movement efficiency resulting in decreased performance and increased risk of injury. If we had today's technology in 1989, it could have helped identify poor movement efficiency and monitor the load to prevent fatigue injuries and build on the endurance factor. We always hear the term core strength. We should use the term core endurance. The ability to keep your center of gravity as the athlete moves through space in an uncontrolled environment. When core stability is lost through fatigue, movement efficiency is lost, and injury risk increases. The idea today is to not break through the wall but to move the wall with good training and monitoring.

In my final years with the Lakers, I had the fortunate circumstance of meeting Dr. Chris Powers from the University of Southern California. Dr. Powers is a trained physical therapist and an associate professor in the Division of Bio-kinesiology. He operates a lab that utilizes the Simi Aktysis system. Through algorithm development and colored LED markers, the system can provide meaningful movement analysis in real-time on video recordings. Powers helped me on more than one occasion to identify athletic biomechanical deficiencies and help correct them. Without Power's input, I'm convinced that athlete would have re-injured himself and possibly endangered his career.

I also invested in the DorsaVi ViPerform wireless sensor technology. The DorsaVi system was designed for athletes to assess injury risk, guide training programs, and determine return to play. The system consists of wearable motion and muscle activity sensors that record data at 200 frames per second. My plan was to assess all players for a baseline in the offseason and prior to training camp. The technology could also be used to monitor load through the season. It could easily be done by putting sensors on one big and one small every practice day.

There are several high-speed camera and high-speed sensor systems today. There are even smart clothes and smart shoes with the sensors incorporated into the garment, so you don't even know it's there. The sensors are actually more sensitive than we need them to be. The technology is in the algorithm. Can the science weed out the noise and the information that the sensor is picking up, but it's not pertinent information.

To know what information is pertinent, you must understand your sport and the demands needed to compete at that level and technology has helped us understand the demands of NBA basketball. Every arena in the NBA is equipped with the Second Spectrum high-speed six-camera system that shoots 25 frames per second. The system recognizes all 13 participants on the playing court, five players on each team and three officials. This technology gives us the number of accelerations and decelerations and the trajectory of each throughout the game.

We can then extrapolate the average speed of each player

and the distance they ran. An equation can then be created to determine load and intensity.

AVERAGE SPEED X DISTANCE X BODY WEIGHT = LOAD
LOAD DIVIDED BY MINUTES PLAYED = INTENSITY

What we were looking for was a direct linear relationship between load and intensity. If load went up, we wanted to see intensity to go up with it. If it did we slotted that individual into a green zone, meaning push training. If intensity began to flatten, then we slotted that individual into a yellow zone, meaning he is on our radar for decreased performance and increased risk of injury which leads us to look closer at the external and internal loads. Obviously, if intensity is crashing, we are probably at a very low-performance state and high injury risk which would require shutting the player down until corrections can be made to meet the needs of the sport.
Arena Technology can objectively measure the demands of an NBA basketball game. Some of these variables include but are not limited to:

LENGTH OF COURT
50ft x 94ft

DIFFERENT SPEEDS THROUGHOUT A GAME
An NBA player runs for about 2 to 4 minutes at a time at an average speed of 3 – 4 MPH but can get up to speeds as high as 14 MPH and as low as barely moving.

DISTANCES RUN THROUGHOUT A GAME:
An NBA player runs approximately 2.5 miles during the course of a game.

TRANSITIONS RUN THROUGHOUT A GAME:
There are generally 10–20 full court transitions throughout a game.

The use of NBA game analytics acquired from using high-speed camera technology coupled with wearable sensor technology for practices can help teams reduce the risk of fatigue injuries like we saw in 1989. The technology is like having another tool in the athletic trainer's toolbox. I think the technology should be looked at in three dimensions:
1. Reinforces something you already know
2. Helps sway you towards a decision that you were on the fence about
3. Alerts you to something you never saw coming

What analytics does not do is measure what's in the heart of a champion. Most people are average, which is the same as saying you are as close to being at the bottom as you are the top. When I would underperform as a child, I always looked at who I did better than. My father asked me why I compared myself to them. Why not compare yourself to those at the top, and he was right.

In the words of the famous Irish poet and playwright, Oscar Wilder: "*Shoot for the moon. Even if you miss, you'll land among the stars.*"

ABOUT THE AUTHOR

Gary Vitti has worked in the health care field for 40 years with 32 of them as the Head Athletic Trainer for the storied Los Angeles Lakers. During his tenure, the team won 14 Division Titles, 12 Conference Titles and 8 NBA Championships. Vitti also represented the Western Conference at 4 All-Star games. He has worked side by side with basketball hall of fame greats Kareem Abdul-Jabbar, Magic Johnson, James Worthy, Shaquille O'Neal , Jamaal Wilkes, Bob McAdoo, Karl Malone, Gary Payton, Mitch Richmond, Dennis Rodman, Bill Sharman, Jerry West, Pat Riley, Phil Jackson and future Hall of Famer Kobe Bryant. From 1984 to 1992 Vitti was also the Head Athletic Trainer for the Los Angeles Strings of World Team Tennis. His teams and exhibition matches included but were not limited to tennis greats Jimmy Connors, John McEnroe, Bjorn Borg, Ivan Lendl, Boris Becker, Martina Navratilova, Billy Jean King, and Chrissy Everett.

In addition to his work experience, Vitti lectures internationally. Since his retirement, he has given the 2019 commencement address to the University of Southern California's Department of Bio-Kinesiology and Physical Therapy along with keynotes including but not limited to the US Military Academy at West Point, The University of Utah College of Health, The Equinox National Forum, Explor Conference, Imaging Network Group Forum and H-Wave's national sales meeting. He has also spoken at conferences in Singapore, Shanghai, Orlando, and Sacramento.

He serves on the board of advisors for the International Sports Academy of Singapore. He has launched an online certification course, written a syndicated column for the LA Times, created an exercise video, published articles in peer-reviewed journals and appeared in two Hollywood movies. He has also been featured in Sports Illustrated, ESPN, ESPN Magazine, ESPN.Com, Fox News Sports, The Doctor's Show, Hoop

Magazine, NBATV, NBA Inside Stuff, CCTV China, Tencent China, and Time Warner Cable Network as well as several other international publications.

Along with his professional life, Vitti is known for his philanthropic work. He created the National Basketball Athletic Trainers Association Foundation which during his tenure as chairman was involved with organ and tissue donation, the Miami Project for paralysis and the National Kidney Foundation as well as providing countless scholarships for young athletic training students. Vitti created the National Athletic Trainers Association Annual Blood Drive (now named in his honor) which set records for convention blood drives for the American Red Cross. He also served on the board of a Window Between Worlds, an organization that uses art as a healing tool for survivors of domestic violence. He currently is on the advisory board of Teamheal and the West Coast Sports Medicine Foundation: organizations that provide health care and education, as well as scholarships in underserved communities and he, is also a strong supporter of the Red Cross, Salvation Army, St. Jude's Hospital and The Boys and Girls Club.

Vitti's work has been recognized and awarded by the 26th US Senate District, the 35th US Congressional District, the City of Los Angeles, the California Legislature, US Naval Medical Center of San Diego, his alma mater Southern Connecti. cut State University, Philippine Sports Commission, NBATA, Loyola Athletics, Teamheal, The West Coast Sports Medicine Foundation, STR Basket Italia, the Kappa Alpha Psi Fraternity and most recently became the national honoree for the Stamford Old Timers Athletic Association.

Vitti has two daughters Rachel and Emilia, a grandson Cole and lives in Manhattan Beach with his wife, Martha.

ACKNOWLEDGMENTS

First and foremost I would like to thank my family. My mom and dad gave my sisters and myself the morals, values and ethics that formed the roots of our success.

My sister Carol for always being my guiding light.

My wife Martha who has supported my personal and career decisions for the last 15 years. Her magnificent family has accepted me and loved me as one of their own.

My daughters Rachel and Emilia who have always lived a life with a true moral compass thanks to their mother, Chris Vitti. I could not have done my job away from my family without knowing there was true stability in the home she created. I'm sure Chris rests in peace knowing her daughters are the true embodiment of the foundation she laid.

I would like to thank my friend Paul Teetor. We had many meetings and exchanged several written versions of 32 years of titles and tears. I had a vision of what I wanted this book to be. Thank you for the help and encouragement to write the book I wanted to write.

Finally, I must thank Rocco Castellano. Without Rocco's publishing knowledge, this book sits in my computer ad infinitum.

CPSIA information can be obtained
at www.ICGtesting.com
Printed in the USA
LVHW052319111219
640173LV00007B/1183/P

9 781686 866708